Understanding Children's Development in the Early Years

Review of the first edition:

'This book provides a very accessible approach to building a better understanding of young children and their development and will be an interesting and useful read for both experienced early years practitioners and for students who are just beginning to build their practical experience.'
– *Early Years Update*

This highly practical and fully updated new edition is full of case studies and helpful advice on how to enhance our understanding of very young children. Through working with many practitioners in different settings, Christine Macintyre offers down-to-earth strategies to enhance the learning of children in their care, and asks:

- What are the key influences in encouraging children to achieve their potential?
- Are the four aspects of children's development equally important and how do they interact?
- Does the play-based curriculum truly cater for children with a range of abilities and interests, such as gifted and talented children and those who need extra support?
- What new ways are there of enhancing learning?
- How can we be sure that parents appreciate how we support their children in all aspects of their development?

With examples and case studies drawn from a variety of real-life early years practices, these interesting and thought-provoking scenarios will help enhance and develop the practice of all students and early years teachers.

Christine Macintyre, formerly a teacher and lecturer at Moray House, Edinburgh University, now works as an early years consultant specialising in the field of movement development. She is currently working with staff who teach children with profound and complex needs and has written many books based on researching developmental issues.

Essential Guides for Early Years Practitioners

Identifying Additional Learning Needs in the Early Years, 2nd Edition
Christine Macintyre
978-1-138-02249-2

Understanding Children's Development in the Early Years, 2nd Edition
Christine Macintyre
978-1-138-02247-8

Music 3–5
Susan Young
978-0-415-43057-9

Thinking and Learning About Mathematics in the Early Years
Linda Pound
978-0-415-43236-8

Supporting Multilingual Learners in the Early Years
Sandra Smidt
978-0-415-43801-8

Essential Nursery Management
Susan Hay
978-0-415-43072-2

Drama 3–5
Debbie Chalmers
978-0-415-42169-0

Understanding Children's Development in the Early Years
Christine Macintyre
978-0-415-41288-9

Helping with Behaviour
Sue Roffey
978-0-415-34291-9

Circle Time for Young Children
Jenny Mosley
978-0-415-34289-6

Identifying Additional Learning Needs in the Early Years
Christine Macintyre
978-0-415-36215-3

Observing, Assessing and Planning for Children in the Early Years
Sandra Smidt
978-0-415-33974-2

Understanding Children's Development in the Early Years

Questions practitioners frequently ask

Second edition

Christine Macintyre

Routledge
Taylor & Francis Group

LONDON AND NEW YORK

Second edition published 2015
by Routledge
2 Park Square, Milton Park, Abingdon, Oxon OX14 4RN

and by Routledge
711 Third Avenue, New York, NY 10017

Routledge is an imprint of the Taylor & Francis Group, an informa business

First edition published by Routledge 2007

British Library Cataloguing in Publication Data
A catalogue record for this book is available from the
British Library

Library of Congress Cataloging in Publication Data
    Macintyre, Christine, 1938-
    Understanding children's development in the early years :
    questions practitioners frequently ask / Christine Macintyre.
    — Second edition.
    pages cm
    1. Education, Preschool. 2. Child development. I. Title.
    LB1140.2.M325 2014
    372.21—dc23
    2013047902

ISBN: 978-1-138-02246-1 (hbk)
ISBN: 978-1-138-02247-8 (pbk)
ISBN: 978-1-317-69019-1 (ebk)

Typeset in Perpetua
by Florence Production Ltd, Stoodleigh, Devon, UK

Printed and bound in the United States of America by Publishers Graphics,
LLC on sustainably sourced paper.

Contents

Illustrations

FIGURES

TABLES

RESOURCES

Acknowledgements

Grateful thanks are offered to all the early years practitioners, the parents and their children who participated in the challenging research that made this book possible. They were unfailingly patient and responsive even when dealing with new ideas e.g. observing not just developing competences in the children – difficult though that is – but monitoring the transfer of learning, i.e. showing how the acquisition of one skill could ease learning others. This involved practitioners in designing learning scenarios where such transfer could be assessed, monitoring the process and evaluating their effectiveness.

A second development was to work on the evaluation of interventions designed to support children who needed extension work or some extra support. These showed how different children responded to similar interventions and they provided a bank of materials that could offer choice to other practitioners, allowing them to consider alternative strategies that could best suit their particular child.

The children in the settings were fascinated by seeing their teachers as learners and they came up with dazzling comments. One child announced he liked buggery best. Well, he'd studied an antery and a wormery, so what else could the study of bugs (minibeasts) be called?

As ever, the early years curriculum based on play allowed the children to thrive and grow, enhancing learning in each aspect of their development. And when some children found playing and learning difficult, there was time to progress at a rate that did not cause stress or indicate that a child was less able than the others in the group. The equal emphasis on all aspects of development also promoted this for there were always chances for each child to shine. This was vitally important for parents as well as the children themselves, and to all of us in education because 'it is to the young that the future belongs'.

Special thanks to Natasha Ellis-Knight at Routledge for her patience and professionalism. She has been unfailingly cheerful and was a marvellous partner in producing this book. Final heartfelt thanks go to the professionals at Routledge who have been meticulous in their care in producing the text. Any mistakes are mine, and I hope you will be kind!

Christine Macintyre

Chapter 1

Setting the scene

Is there anything more intriguing and important than discovering how children come to be as they are and how we can support them as they develop so many skills and understandings? This is a complex undertaking due to the individual nature of children. Many are lively, full of excitement and promise, highly motivated to learn and confident with expectations and resolutions of their own while others are timid, distressed and reluctant to join in activities and learn new things and there are all shades in between. But understanding them all is particularly important for this is their fastest learning time. As long ago as 1977, Professor Colwyn Trevarthen made a number of claims that help practitioners justify the importance of the work they do. This is important as it is sometimes difficult to summarise such a complex endeavour. He wrote:

- The brain of every child in every culture goes through the same developmental stages.
- Children learn 50 per cent of everything they know in the first five years.
- Children are intrinsically motivated to learn.
- Curiosity is needed to develop the brain.
- Children need the right experiences at the right time.

The first claim eases observation in a multi cultural setting, explaining as it does that development follows the same pattern in all children. Yet practitioners have still to discover what stage each child is at and how they prefer to learn. They realise that although the stages are the same, not all children will reach the same level of achievement and the rate of progress will be different. The second claim is huge but doesn't hold surprises for those experienced in interacting with young children. They are constantly delighted by the ways children expand their understandings and visibly grow in stature before their eyes. Few children lack curiosity but planning the best experiences to encourage their abilities and skills can be challenging. Listening to the children and finding their preferred ways of tackling problems could be useful ploys i.e. by cueing in to their interests and really listening to what they have to say. Given that they are primed to learn, it can be a rewarding experience to find that most children can not only respond to the learning experiences they encounter, but make choices and find innovative and creative responses.

Some children appear to have every advantage. Even being big for their age has certain benefits. While at first sight this may seem strange and presumptuous, Bee and Boyd (2005) claim that stature makes a big difference to children being popular and competent. This is because other children tend to look up to those who are 'big' and this is often reinforced by adults giving them more challenges and greater responsibility. And when expectations are higher, the children raise their game. Little children tend to be more sheltered with adults often doing things they could manage themselves! There is an important message for adults here.

If children come from advantaged backgrounds they will be likely to have more physical resources in terms of books and more opportunities to experience cultural events. However these things may come at the cost of having less quality time with parents or freedom to play so the different potentials need to be carefully considered by families in the knowledge of their child. Unfortunately, many children from less well-to-do homes do not begin their education on a level playing field. In some families 'other concerns', perhaps financial, perhaps health issues detract from the attention that can be given to the children. These differences have to be understood when studying the impact of the nurture/environmental side of development. Many practitioners give time and resources to compensate for any lack. Some children from advantaged and some from disadvantaged backgrounds will be gifted and talented, the latter group probably overcoming hurdles to shine, but many do!

Yet another group of children have special needs or in the newer term learning differences and these impact on learning if memorising or organising (intellectual difficulties) or movement/social/emotional difficulties restrict what children can do. A smaller but sadly increasing number have profound disabilities such as autistic spectrum disorders that hinder their ability to participate in many activities. (The ratios for autism have moved from 1:1000–1:100 children (Moore 2012)). A great deal of preparation needs to happen to enable these children to make the most of their time in school.

Even children in the same family can be 'chalk and cheese' with one child athletic and extrovert, another musical and shy and a third aggressive and moody. These differences must suggest nature or inherited differences rather than nurture or environmental ones since the upbringing has been largely the same. However Carter (2000) explains that even with twins, minute differences in the womb can cause differences. Whatever the reason, the differences indicate that each child requires a different level and kind of support. Parents and practitioners wonder, 'Why should this be?' 'How can I best communicate with each of these very different children?' 'How will I discover what each child's needs are?' and 'How can I plan the most stimulating learning opportunities to enhance each child's profile?' Finding answers is the constant concern of all the adults that interact with the children as they recognise the responsibility they have in nurturing them in this, the fastest learning time. For this is the time when the brain is most ready to learn. In the early years, the children's brains are 'plastic' i.e. most responsive in terms of absorbing and adapting to different kinds of input. Young brains are intrinsically curious to learn, primed to make the new and vital connections between neurons (brain cells) that allow new skills and creative abilities to develop. Early years education at home and at nursery or children and families' centres aims to nurture these early potentials, hopefully through providing a curriculum based on play. At the same time a process called maturation ensures that basic skills such as walking and speaking develop too. Maturational skills are intrinsic to development. In children without difficulties they do not need to be taught.

When children come to early years settings for the first time, practitioners focus on welcoming both them and their families so that the beginning of a social bond is formed. Then, over time they observe and assess how each child matches all the milestones of the different aspects of development. But as children are such individual young people, making sense of what they choose to do and recognising the progress therein is a daunting task. This is especially so as development is not a smooth path – it comes in stops and starts, but although children find they are more competent in some areas than others, there is a sense that the different aspects of development blossom together. (See Table 1.1 and Appendices 1 and 2 for more information on developmental milestones.)

TABLE 1.1 Developmental progress in three key areas

Play	Language	Movement
5 years Can initiate or join in role play.	Can follow a story without pictures. Can read simple words.	Can run and jump, ride a bike and zip a coat. Understands the rules of major games.
4 years Understands pretence and develops fears of the unknown. Develops imaginative games, not always able to explain rules.	Knows colours and numbers. Can explain events, hopes and disappointments. Able to listen and focus.	Can climb and swing on large apparatus. Has a developed sense of safety outdoors. Can swim. Enjoys bunny jumps and balancing activities.
3 years Enjoys group activities e.g. baking a cake for someone's birthday. Understands turn taking.	Uses complex sentences. Understands directional words and simple comparisons e.g. big/small.	Can ride a trike and climb stairs. Climbs in and out of cars/buses independently. Can catch a large ball.
2.5 years Develops altruism especially for family members. Understands emotional words e.g. happy, sad.	Uses pronouns and past tenses adding 'ed' to form own version of past tense.	Uses a step-together pattern to climb stairs. Can walk some distance.
2 years Beginning to play alongside a friend for a short time (parallel play).	Rebels – says 'No'. Can form two word sentences but comprehension is far ahead of speech.	Can walk well but jumping is still difficult. Climbs on furniture (crawling pattern).
18 months Sensorimotor play exploring the properties of objects (solitary play).	Has 10 naming words. Points to make wishes known.	Can crawl at speed and walk but jumping is not developed. Balance is precarious!
1 year Walks unsteadily, arms and step pattern wide to help balance.	Enjoys games e.g. peek-a-boo. Beginning to enjoy books and stories. Monosyllabic babbling.	Plays with toys giving them correct usage – simple pretend e.g. feeding doll.
6–8 months Can sit unsupported briefly. Rolls over. Attempts to crawl.	Makes sounds and blows bubbles.	Reaching out for objects now. Changing objects from one hand to the other.
0–4 months May be able to support head but weight of head makes this difficult. Strength developing head to toe and centre to periphery. Can lift head briefly in front lying.	Early communication: responds to voices: can make needs known.	Plays with hands as first toy. Can hold object placed in hand but cannot let go – object drops.

But of course it is one thing having charts, another to be able to 'see' what is going on. This takes experience, a clear idea of what is to be observed, a record of developmental changes and an intervention plan when challenges need to be extended or when there are developmental blips.

Since accurate observation and assessment is so challenging, having a structure to aid the process can be achieved by studying the four aspects of development separately, always remembering two things. The first is that other factors such as heredity and maturation (genetic influences) and cultural mores and resources (environmental influences) play a significant part in the process of development. The second is that although the four aspects are separated out to allow focus, they do constantly intertwine with progress in one affecting all of the others too. This can be shown in diagrammatic form (Figure 1.1).

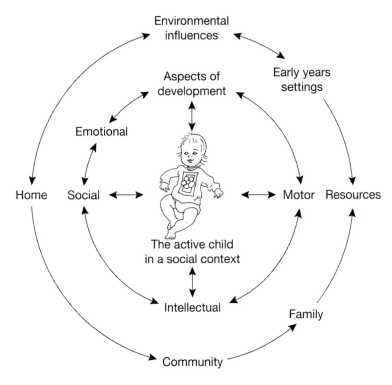

FIGURE 1.1 Different aspects of development

The four aspects of development, i.e. motor, social, emotional and intellectual, prompt a number of age-related questions to guide observations. These are:

1. **Motor** or movement. Have the children reached their motor milestones? (See Appendix 1.) Do they appear to be strong or are they floppy? Can they crawl using the cross lateral pattern, walk without stumbling, handle early years equipment safely and even for a short spell, can they be still? Are they willing to venture onto apparatus such as a low bench and can they balance there? Do they demonstrate that they are strong enough to carry out the age-appropriate skills of daily living e.g. carrying plates of food at snack without spilling or getting their coats on without help? Is there any strange pattern when they walk? (A strange gait can be an early sign of difficulties and should be monitored closely to find if maturation 'works' or if further scrutiny is necessary. Walking on tiptoes often causes concern but usually disappears without expert help. Still, it should be recorded and monitored).

2. **Social.** Do the children respond to others, both adults and children, initiate 'conversations' with eye contact, gestures or words, gradually make friends with their peers and appear willing to join in a game? Will they stay without their parents without distress? Do they understand they will return later? Will they take hands in a circle and sit near different children? Do they show they are interested in what others are doing or saying? Do they welcome approaches from others or shrug them off showing resentment or simply ignore what is going on? At 3 years, are they willing to share resources, will they wait for a turn? At 4 years, do they understand and appreciate that other children can be distressed/hurt even although they themselves are happy?

   N.B. Special attention needs to be given if a child does not respond when their name is called. If this happens, try calling again in a lighthearted way and record how the child responds. Consistent ignoring needs to be investigated and recorded along with observations of how they play with toys and if they give a toy a character.

3. **Emotional.** Have they shown attachment behaviours/built a bond with someone in the setting? Do they show increasing

confidence in speaking to an adult or another child? Can they settle quickly after changes in routine? Are they confident and willing to meet new challenges? Will they 'have a go'? And if they don't manage, do they get upset, even freak out or are they willing to listen to suggestions and try again? Do they show concern for others if they are hurt or sad? Can they cope with sudden changes in routine or friendship patterns? If they are sad, can they be comforted quite readily or do they simmer and sulk and behave aggressively as a result?

Are they aggressive towards others? This is an important observation as even early years children can bully others. It is important to remember that bullying is repeated nasty behaviour – not a one-off occurrence.

4. **Intellectual.** Can the children listen to a short story or poem? Do they remember from one day to the next? Can they concentrate for a spell on something they have chosen to do? Are they interested in stories and can they remember simple sequences? Are they imaginative in their play scenarios? Do they enjoy finding out or problem solving? Do they take the initiative in trying something new? Can they focus on a task and concentrate for a short time or do they flit from activity to activity without completing anything? Are they willing to dress up – do they understand its purpose?

N.B. A key question: can the children transfer what they have learned to help them in another situation? This is very important as the transfer, often called habituation, eases learning in a new context. As the ability to transfer is at the root of intelligent behaviour, should ideas for potential transfers be part of planning observations and recordings?

UNDERSTANDING HABITUATION AND TRANSFER OF LEARNING: EXTENDING OBSERVATIONS IN MOTOR SKILLS

Think about children coming down stairs. After the sliding down on tummy, feet first stage, the children will use a tentative step-together action with two feet on each step, but gradually once confidence and balance is gained the single passing step pattern with no need to hold on is achieved. Most children will be able to adapt this skill so that when they meet different stairways with different risers, they competently, almost instinctively cope with the change. This is habituation. Children who can't habituate – children with Dyspraxia fall into this category – must learn each step pattern as a first time try. This takes time and effort in coping with the different context. The skill doesn't seem to get passed on but stays as an isolated skill. So practitioners observing children should record not only discrete skills but later, once practiced, find whether it has 'worked' or enabled competence in another context i.e. whether transfer of learning has occurred.

This is important in all aspects of learning. In intellectual learning does appreciating the sequence of one story lead to them being able to anticipate the possible development of events in another? Can they respond to 'what do you think might happen now?' Do they recognise that the number 2 on the snack table helps them count apples into a basket or is the sign in the 'one, two' rhymes? Understanding this would help the children understand that an abstract symbol has meaning. Could they suggest times when the colour red means 'stop'?

Perhaps more time spent on this kind of explanation would help transfer to be achieved?

In social learning, has 'recognising how to make a friend indoors' helped them communicate with children in the larger play area outside? Has tending to dolls in the hospital area enabled them to empathise when friends get hurt? Do stories about sharing lead to them being willing to share at play? Do talks on healthy eating in the setting make them prefer healthy foods at snack time or at home?

And emotionally do the children recognise that they can pass on the comfort/support they have received to understand the difficulties of another child? Do the children love being praised and does this help them to be more confident in tackling something new? If they are reassured that Mum is coming back shortly does this help them to settle or are they still anxious?

Observations of transfer of learning are difficult to see and record but they are significant in defining intelligent behaviour. My own favourite definition of intelligent behaviour is 'being able to act appropriately in different situations' and at its root that must involve transfer.

WHEN TRANSFER DOESN'T OCCUR

One teacher who had taught a child with dyspraxia to swim was astounded to be asked, 'Can you come home with me now and teach me to swim in my pool?' The child had no notion that she had achieved a transferable skill. So explanations e.g. 'Look, this is nearly the same, we can use or do this over here' may be needed alongside praising achievements. Transfer is difficult in dyspraxia but the children have the capacity to understand and gradually they can learn to do this. This is helped by examples being spelt out e.g. 'When we played a game with the bands, the red one meant? Yes, Stop! Now look at the traffic lights on the road outside. When the red light shines, what do the cars do?' And follow this with other examples of red for danger. Unfortunately children at the more profound end of the autistic spectrum, living as they do in the here and now, find transfer impossible. They can't visualise future events and probably won't wait for or pay heed to explanations. But for most other children pointing out where transfer occurs could be a very helpful and interesting way to help them recognise habituation.

And as practitioners record such developments they become fascinated by the way the different aspects of development interact e.g. the children's confidence and self-esteem rises as they learn to climb on the frame or master baking for snack or remember colours learned the day before. This encourages them to tackle something new and to try again when new activities are difficult. However some children can be overwhelmed by overt praise and prefer a smile or a thumbs up sign. This is another reason why practitioners have to know their children so well.

As these developments unfold and often in discussion with interested parents, staff prepare learning opportunities to nurture each child's individual profile of abilities and skills. In this way gifts and difficulties are recognised and provide evidence for planning interventions that offer extension material or additional support. If outstanding abilities are apparent or difficulties persist, then outside experts are often called in to give a specific diagnosis and provide programmes of support. This reassures parents that everything is being done to foster each child's progress.

It is fascinating to find that 'the three Rs' still lead planning now. Long ago the initials stood for 'Rhetoric, Reading and Religion'. This was a time when the curriculum was set and children had to get to grips with it or fail. There was no appreciation of or room for deviance and few opportunities for being creative. Later, in everyday usage, the 'three Rs' came to mean 'Reading, Writing and Arithmetic' but this notation was still limiting as those three subjects were given the most prominence, suggesting a hierarchy that devalued the Arts and Sciences – and the spelling was suspect, was it not? Today they stand for 'Respect, Relationships and Responsive care'. This vast change in philosophy means that the early years environment aims to make each child feel valued and secure, to give an all-round experience of learning through a play based curriculum, nurturing as this does the social, emotional, creative and motor abilities of the children as well as the intellectual ones. This allows development in all the activities of daily living and should foster caring, compassionate and competent children. Within the groups of children nominated as being 'gifted,' more subtle and hard to assess abilities such as leadership or producing creative responses are being given prominence. In the earliest years the strategies children use to gain attention might make useful observations. Could this be a sign of 'knowingness' and might that develop into something special? Parents finding their lives are taken over by their demanding youngsters might be comforted by the thought!

Chapter 2

The very beginning of learning

Many early years settings in the different sectors now have baby rooms and playrooms where babies and toddlers are cared for and so the expertise of the staff must embrace the needs of tiny children. For these practitioners and arguably for all early years specialists, 'understanding child development' has to start at conception, because that's when babies begin and influences on their development happen too. This is the time when the nature part of development is set, yet nurture in terms of the quality of the first environment, the womb and later other environments (physical, social, intellectual and emotional) are vitally important too. From the outset nature and nurture work together to fashion the child and the proportional influence of each is the subject of much research. For practitioners, the understanding that their support for babies, toddlers and youngsters can foster high abilities, encourage 'average' children and support less fortunate children to help them overcome the effects of a poor start is highly motivating. But this is also a massive responsibility. So how can practitioners nurture all their children who come from different backgrounds and who have their own preferences, temperaments and competences? Perhaps through finding answers to questions such as, 'Why are children all so different? 'When do they begin to learn and acquire all the skills of daily living? 'How do they change as time goes by?' And importantly for justifying the importance of early education, 'Are the earliest experiences and opportunities the children have really the building blocks of later learning?' Let's find out how this amazing development happens by starting at the beginning and looking at the process of development from there.

CONCEPTION

At conception a single sperm from the millions produced by the male travels through the vagina, cervix, uterus and fallopian tube to pierce the wall of the ovum (i.e. the egg from the female). And so a child is conceived. Both the father's sperm and the mother's egg (the gametes) contain genes and these combine to create an individual profile for this child. This is known as the genotype. A second or subsequent child will inherit different genes because a different sperm and egg have come together at conception. These genes carry characteristics such as hair colour, height, body shape, temperament and aspects of intelligence and also the maturational processes that determine the patterns of physical and intellectual development.

In the nucleus of each cell in the body there are 46 chromosomes but the sperm and the ovum (the gametes) have only 23 each so that when they come together 46 are present. And because each child inherits two of each chromosome (one from each parent), the genetic instructions may be the same (homozygous) or different (heterozygous). Sometimes when they are different the two appear to blend. Children of one tall and one small parent generally have a final height somewhere between the two and the child who receives an A-type blood code from one parent and a B-type from the other will have an AB type. But more often one gene is dominant and the other recessive. The recessive gene can stay dormant in the child but be passed on to the next generation (that is why families are amazed to see 'granny's gestures and preferences' all over again) but only the dominant one determines the characteristics of the conceived child.

A number of inherited diseases such as cystic fibrosis or disabilities e.g. autism, ADHD (Attention Deficit Hyperactivity Disorder) can emerge 'unexpectedly' if parents both have recessive genes that hold that disorder. A carrier is someone who inherits the disease gene from one parent. Such a person does not have the disease but can pass it on if their partner also has the recessive gene.

Most human characteristics are affected by a multitude of genes. The child's growth pattern, intelligence, eye colour (brown is dominant over blue) and temperament all involve the interaction of several genes. Helen Bee (2010) calls this, 'the genetic blueprint' and to some extent this influences what the child will be able to do.

However no geneticist would claim that inherited genes fully determine what the child will become. While the genotype is the set of 'instructions' contained in an individual's genes, the phenotype is the name given to observed characteristics and is the product of three components, the genotype, environmental influences from the moment of conception on and the interaction between the genotype and the environment. So a potentially highly intelligent foetus may be damaged by the expectant mother drinking too much alcohol or taking drugs and damaging the nervous system of the child. And if the mum should contract rubella in the first three months of pregnancy, the child's sight and hearing could be affected. Most organ systems develop rapidly in the first twelve weeks and this is the time when they are vulnerable to the effect of teratogens or harmful substances. Every child is affected by the quality of its very first environment, i.e. the quality of the sustenance provided by the womb.

Goddard (2006) and Bee and Boyd (2005) have found that many more noxious substances than previously thought pass through the umbilical cord to harm the foetus, damaging the developing brain and resulting in birth difficulties e.g. foetal alcohol syndrome or the babies enduring a lengthy withdrawal from drugs. There are of course other difficulties that occur despite optimum conditions in the womb. For some conditions that infer learning difficulties e.g. Down's syndrome and autistic spectrum disorders are already present before birth. The latter may be hidden until age 2.5 or so when language and communication skills do not develop in the usual way and when expectations put pressure on the child. Cerebral palsy may be present pre-natally or be caused by severe birth problems. These understandings can help parents be ready in emotional and practical terms and give practitioners time to ensure that the necessary support in terms of specific resources or more detailed understanding of the child's condition is in place before they come to the setting. This preparation also helps the staff to appreciate any difficulties in the home when there are disabled children and allows them to give more time to listen to parents and empathise with them, perhaps sharing their appreciation for the way that they manage their day, assisting them whenever they can and working together to share plans for the child's progress.

Researchers often try to gauge whether the genetic aspect is more powerful than the environmental one by studying identical twins who have been separated early on. The findings show that the IQs of the twins and often their lifestyles remain markedly similar even when they have been brought up in different countries and have never met. So does 'what children inherit' really control what they can achieve? This research suggests that this is so. However, some children from disadvantaged homes with low achieving parents or harrowing disabilities overcome seemingly insurmountable barriers and do extremely well while their seemingly more advantaged peers falter and underachieve. So motivated children, anxious to learn, *can* overcome disadvantaged environments. Appropriate timely intervention and support does make a huge difference to the outcome. Practitioners setting out to maximise the educational chances for all of their children plan learning opportunities believing that this is the case.

Parents and practitioners can make good early disadvantages too. A potentially aggressive child may be mellowed by sensitive and patient adults who take time to demonstrate and explain other ways of behaving and a 'slow-to-participate' one may overcome worries about joining in by consistent praise and encouragement. In addition, practitioners can usefully model the way they would like the children to behave. In the pressures of a busy day often with conflicting demands, this can be very difficult, yet must be given priority. They will remember of course that children on the autistic spectrum won't be able to copy their behaviour. They don't learn from others as they lack a theory of mind, i.e. the ability to understand the thoughts, emotions and feelings of another person. Practitioners can also ensure that all children enjoy respect and an equal share of attention when designing and explaining learning opportunities. Sharing this ideal encourages parents to cooperate in revealing home observations that are so useful for planning inputs based on children's interests.

THE NEWBORN CHILD

The newborn child is assessed at birth and again five minutes later using the Apgar score. The baby is scored on five categories and given a score of 0, 1 or 2 on each. A score of ten is fairly unusual immediately after birth but at five minutes 85–90 per cent attain this score. A score of 7 or more indicates that there are no problems, 4, 5 or 6 can mean support with breathing is indicated and a low score of 3 or less shows that the baby is in a critical condition although many do survive, catch up with their peer group and do very well.

THE EARLIEST ASSESSMENT OF CHILDREN

The first assessments of children come through observing their motor skills e.g. if and when they were able to support their heads, when they sat, reached out and grasped, when they crawled and stood and walked.

TABLE 2.1 The Apgar score

Aspect of infant observed	Score 0	Score 1	Score 2
Heart rate	Absent	< 100 min	> 100 min
Respiratory rate	No breathing	Weak cry and shallow breathing	Strong cry and regular breathing
Muscle tone	Flaccid	Some flexion of fingers and toes	Well flexed
Response to a stimulus	None	Some movement	Cry
Colour	Blue: Pale	Body pink Extremities blue	Pink all over

Source: Francis et al. (1987)

These are the foundations of later learning. Sally Goddard (1996) who writes extensively on the importance of movement and the underlying reflexes explains:

All later learning is based upon the motor skills that develop during our first year of life. The reflexes form a checks-and-balance system. If they are present and active at the correct time, then the account remains in credit. If they are undeveloped or persist beyond the correct time they form a debit and they may extract a price later from higher levels of brain functioning.

So what are these reflexes?

Reflexes in the newborn

Reflexes are involuntary movements i.e. not triggered by conscious control. There are different types. First, the *adaptive reflexes* that help the baby survive e.g. the sucking and swallowing reflexes and the rooting reflex that ensures the baby turns towards the nipple in feeding following a touch on the cheek. Less useful perhaps is the grasping reflex (an evolutionary reflex needed by apes allowing them to cling to their mothers as they swing in the jungle); however this strong action in babies can please parents and grandparents who love to have a finger held by the baby. They see it as a sign of strength and development, even communication. Perhaps if it helps bonding, it is useful after all?

Second there are primitive reflexes, so called because they are controlled by the medulla and the midbrain, areas that are close to full development at birth. After six months or so, when the brain has more fully developed the capacity for perception, movement control and thinking, these should be washed away allowing postural reflexes to emerge. If these primitive reflexes endure they can prevent more sophisticated actions taking place. And so assessing the status of reflexes that are present can indicate neurological wellbeing or delay. Just three that are particularly relevant to the early years setting will be explained here. (For an in-depth study, read Goddard (1996)).

The MORO reflex

One sequence of particular interest to practitioners in early years settings is the MORO reflex because it can explain why some children are stressed and often hypersensitive to sounds, smells, lights and noises causing them to react inappropriately.

It is important that practitioners understand this reflex because, as Goddard (1996) claims 'While other residual reflexes tend to have an impact on specific skills, it is the MORO which has an overall effect on the emotional profile of the child.'

After birth this reflex acts as an alarm and it comes into play if loud noises or sudden changes, e.g. dropping the baby's head below the level of the spine, distress the child. Babies will arch their backs, throw their arms wide and take a sudden gasp of air and for a moment 'freeze' before the arms cross back and the spine relaxes. This is an involuntary response to a threat. The MORO reflex also plays a part in developing the breathing mechanism and helps 'arousal', if for example a blanket falls over the baby's face. This reflex should be inhibited at 3 months of neonate life and be replaced by the adult startle reflex. If not, the children can be hypersensitive in some areas of sensory perception. Their hearing may be confused by oversensitivity to specific sounds. They will be distressed by bright lights, strong smells e.g. soap in the sink, even cooking or perfume smells and may run from the source of upset. Hand driers and toilet flushes can be intolerable. This tension stimulates high levels of adrenalin and cortisol, the stress hormones, so feelings are over-reactive and the children are wired to escape. They need to be able to reduce this tension to allow them to concentrate on learning.

Sutherland (2008) explains that cortisol 'at base levels is necessary for learning and for helping the body deal with stress,' but 'when it is retained for too long then the frontal lobes in the brain get flushed with stress chemicals and thinking is geared to threat'. So if Mum's return is delayed, if changes in routine become overwhelming, or if the children consider they can't cope, i.e. if levels of cortisol don't return to base, the distressed children can't think logically or apply reason. They can't calm themselves down.

So what is to be done? Sutherland offers a way forward in what she calls 'The key relational needs of the child'. These she describes as

1) Attunement where the adult strives to appreciate the child's emotional intensity and uses this to connect with the child.
2) Validation of how the child is experiencing the event. This requires the adult to affirm and understand the child's distress and use the correct tone of voice and body posture to convey empathy.
3) Containment of feelings. This involves the adult appreciating the child's intense feelings but staying calm, not becoming angry. However Sutherland advises that there should be 'house rules' with consequences to prevent the children becoming what she calls 'limit deprived'.
4) Soothing (tension regulation). This means that adults calm the children through staying calm and empathising with the children. This role modeling will help the children, over time, to self-regulate their behaviour.

These pieces of advice are very useful pointers for ways to interact when children are stressed and tense. In addition, having a quiet corner where children can look out, even stand and stare for a time can prevent the reflex, often called the 'fight or flight reflex', taking over and forcing the child to behave in an aggressive or withdrawing manner.

The palmar reflex

This is the reflex that stimulates grasping. If the baby's palm is touched the fingers will close, sometimes very firmly! This reflex should be active for the first three months after birth. This should then be replaced by the pincer grip by 6 months. It is a development of the pointing action – children on the autistic spectrum are not likely to use pointing because

FIGURE 2.1 Lily is fascinated by 'Round and round the garden' and wishes to share her game with Dad. The pointing action helps develop her pincer grip.

they don't realise that someone else doesn't know what they know – so why would they need to be shown?

Often children at early years settings will still use a whole hand/palmar grasp to hold a pencil or paint brush, thus limiting their range of action and the accuracy of colouring or painting. The palmar reflex is still active and inhibiting dexterity. In the early months there is a link between the palmar reflex and feeding, seen when the babies open and close their fingers as they suck and some older children who have retained this reflex will 'write with their tongues' or show other mouthing movements as they scribe. If this reflex is not inhibited, acquiring the pincer grip will be very difficult, needing the children's total concentration: the thumb will stay underused and coordinated actions, even speech, may be negatively affected.

Some songs (e.g. Peter pointer) ask children to focus their attention on their index finger and activities such as drawing patterns in the sand do this too. All hand strengthening activities e.g. rolling clay, mixing colours or flour, are useful. Any activity that provides some resistance – even swirling fingers through deep water – will help. Old fashioned ditties e.g. 'Here is the church, here is the steeple' and of course 'Round and round the garden' are useful because they can focus the children's attention on their hands and so help self-awareness.

Recognising the difficulties that are implicit in having a retained palmar reflex also brings to light why, for many, even most children, formal writing is not appropriate in the early years setting. Practitioners and parents have to wait till maturation and practice strengthens small fingers and allows this complex activity to be achieved.

The asymmetric tonic neck reflex

Another fascinating reflex with massive implications for learning is the asymmetric tonic neck reflex (ATNR). During life in the womb, movement of the baby's head to one side elicits a stretch of the arm to that side and flexion of the other. This action stimulates the kicking action and so promotes muscle strength and aids the vestibular sense, helping balance. It actually helps the baby to twist down the birth canal when being born. At around six months however, the developing brain should stimulate different patterns that inhibit this reflex. If this doesn't happen, if the ATNR is not inhibited, it will inhibit the development of skills, particularly those that involve crossing the midline of the body.

A key developmental skill is being able to crawl using the cross lateral pattern, i.e. one hand and the opposite knee forward. A child with a retained ATNR will find this impossible – so carefully observing the ability to crawl is critically important. Homolateral crawling (the hand and knee on the same side going forward) will not do. Crawling and creeping are important for the development of hand-eye coordination, for the development of balance and for all skills that require crossing the midline of the body. These include fastening buttons, turning a page, writing, reading, using a knife and fork, throwing and kicking a ball, in fact many of the activities of daily living. Even reading can be affected because in the cross-lateral pattern the children will follow their hands with their eyes and so learn to control their vision at reading distance.

When children have difficulties in carrying out actions that others do with ease, it may be that they have missed the developmental sequence that would have caused their reflexes to be inhibited. So the children must retrace their steps as it were and practise these movements for short spells every single day. This gives their brain a second chance. More practice of the things they cannot do will not help the basic issue to be resolved.

19

Crawling using the cross-lateral pattern is just one key example of an early pattern that has profound implications for later learning.

CHANGES IN GROWTH AND MOVEMENT ABILITY FROM BIRTH – 18 MONTHS

During this period babies make remarkable changes. Development is very fast. Development moves from the head downwards (cephalo caudal) and from the centre to periphery (proximo distal). This explains why babies can hold their heads before they sit and sit before they crawl and why pointing and letting go i.e. actions at the extremities, come after being able to hold the trunk erect.

But accompanying changes in the nervous system happen too. At birth the medulla and the midbrain are the most completely developed parts. They regulate all the basic tasks such as paying attention, sleeping, waking, elimination and movement of the head and neck. The least well-developed part of the brain is the cerebral cortex, the wrinkled grey matter that wraps around the midbrain and deals with perception, movement and language and all complex thinking such as problem solving.

The brain has many different parts that work together to allow us to laugh and to cry, to bond with family members, to understand what is happening around us, to learn language and other skills that are necessary for daily living and to make creative moves that extend thinking and

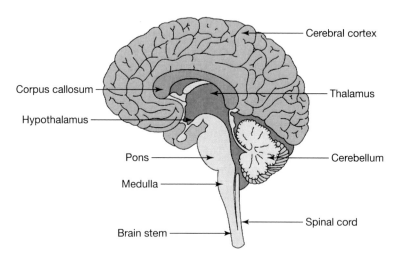

FIGURE 2.2 The brain

rationalising and decision making. But all of this cannot happen at once. The brain needs time to mature. Winston (2004), investigating impulsivity in children, selected 'delayed gratification' as a research topic. He assured children offered one sweet that if they waited to taste it until later, they would be given a second. Despite the bribe, he found that many could not wait. The reward centre in the frontal cortex was immature and could not rationalise waiting for a prize! In many children the reward centre does not mature till adulthood. This is especially so in children with ADHD (Attention Deficit Hyperactivity Disorder) who engage in obsessive, even dangerous behaviour because the impulse to move is not controlled by the reward centre. But when this part of the brain matures, as adolescents they can be much calmer, not driven to act as they were in their younger years.

At birth the baby is dependent on the brain stem, with some input from the midbrain and the cerebellum at the back of the brain. This area, often called the little brain because it is in two parts like the cortex, controls muscle tone. The relative helplessness of the new baby, for example in being unable to reach out, shows how immature strength/muscle tone is. These 'lower brain' parts control vital functions such as regulating breathing, blood pressure and the general level of alertness so necessary for survival. Only gradually through maturation do other parts become active.

Linked to the brain stem is the reticular activating system (RAS). This is a complex bundle of nerve fibres that monitor sensory signals causing them to stimulate or calm sensations in different situations. This is vital in maintaining consciousness and arousal. The limbic system is made up of different areas e.g. the amygdala (the seat of negative emotions), the hypothalamus (involved with memory and learning) and part of the thalamus (a relay station between the cortex and the sensory organs). They are all associated with learning memory and emotional processing.

The midbrain forms a bridge connecting the lower structures to the cerebral cortex. It holds the hypothalamus, the basal ganglia and the thalamus and these centres, along with the cerebellum, organise the motor, sensory and autonomic systems. They are important in the planning and organising of actions.

At the back is the cerebellum or little brain. Although it can't initiate movement on its own, it controls muscle tone and monitors all the impulses from the motor centres in the brain and from nerve endings (proprioceptors) in the muscles. It coordinates all the input from the senses thus controlling every movement. Information from the vestibular sense (balance), from the eyes and from the lower limbs and trunk all pass through the cerebellum en route to their specialist area for analysis and action. The cerebellum is also critically important in the development of myelin, a coating around the axons that eases the accurate transmission of messages between neurones (see Figure 2.2).

At the top of the brain is the cerebral cortex, divided into two hemispheres and linked by the corpus collosum. Most tasks involve both hemispheres with signals passing rapidly through the corpus collosum (a bundle of millions of nerve fibres) so utilising the competences that are housed in the two parts. This part can be 40 per cent larger in women – hence their ability to multi task – and smaller in men, determining their single mindedness! Children with some learning differences, e.g. dyspraxia, have smaller ones too explaining perhaps their difficulties with slick organisation and limited dexterity. In gifted children the corpus collosum is large, facilitating learning.

The right hemisphere appears to be 'the practice ground' for learning new skills that then pass to the left side for refinement. In learning to read for example, the brain activity happens mainly in the right hemisphere but at 7 years or so the learning shifts to the left for attention to detail and logic (Bakker 1990). This is one reason why Nordic countries delay formal education till age 7. By then the children are ready for more complex input especially as they have built a foundation of other skills and abilities e.g. skiing, outward bound activities. These give confidence and strength and in building neurological connections facilitate all kinds of learning.

'Proper language' begins in the second year with activation of the two speech areas that are both in the left side of the brain. Broca's area deals with speech articulation while Wernicke's area deals with comprehension. These two areas together with a bridge between them, the insula, should work in concert. However in some children with hyperlexia, Broca's area is in overdrive with the other, Wernicke's, not functioning well. So the children talk without understanding what they are saying. This is unusual as the development of comprehension usually precedes speech. And in dyslexia, it has been found that the insula does not 'fire' as it should (Carter 2000) so that children have a physical cause for their language problems.

Each hemisphere is split into four lobes. At the back, the occipital lobe is mainly made up of the visual processing area. The parietal lobe at the top copes with movement, orientation and recognition and the temporal lobe deals with sound, comprehension and memory. The frontal lobes deal with executive thinking, problem solving, conceptualisation and planning. Physical, social and emotional development matures alongside the intellectual aspect.

The neurons

The cells that create activity in the brain are neurones. At birth babies have 100 billion neurones but they are not yet mature as the axons or parts that convey the messages or instructions have not grown. The information from the senses is received by the dendrites, passed along the axon and then crosses the synapse to connect with other receiving cells on surrounding neurons. Development comes when the axons grow and become myelinated and neurones work together. Neurones are grey cells (the thinking cells that Poirot often mentions) and they are supported by white or glial cells that insulate the axons. This is myelin and it develops in phases.

In infancy there are two major phases of brain development. At 2 or 3 months of age there is a rapid development of synaptic connections. These are 'experience-expectant' synapses that are preparing the brain to receive new experiences. The second phase at 2+ years is the development of 'experience-dependent' synapses. These are dependent on environmental experiences in order to be activated. There is another

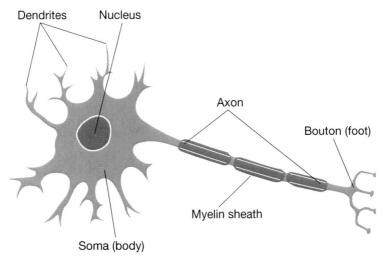

FIGURE 2.3 A neuron

surge at age 6–7 when the children become able for more complex tasks. These observations are important for the timing of planning teaching materials. The nature–nurture interaction is evident again!

BUT WHAT IS LEARNING?

Throughout the text 'learning' is a key concept. But what happens when children learn and how do parents and practitioners know that learning has taken place?

Learning has occurred when children know something new or can do something they couldn't manage before. If there is no change, there has been no learning. But is it possible for children to be in a social, interactive environment and learn nothing? It seems that learning occurs most easily when what has to be learned is just one step beyond what the children already know. This means that expectations are realistic and success is possible. The children can appreciate what is to be achieved and know they will be able to do it too. Genuine praise can then happen, the children's self-esteem can rise and they can anticipate new tasks with confidence. Parents and practitioners who are role models have to remember to display the characteristics they would like to see emerge in their children. In very busy days this can be hard to do! But children learn through osmosis, by absorbing the unsaid as well as or even more than the verbal instructions they hear. Facial expressions and body language convey 90 per cent of the message – where these disagree with the spoken word, this is called metaincongruence and is the source of confusion for the children. Practitioners can unwittingly do this when for example they look at a child's art work, say 'Wonderful' and look over to a group of children who are being noisy, giving a 'calm down gesture' and then move off to settle a squabble. The artist feels belittled and possibly reluctant to try again.

The idea of new learning being just one step beyond the children's competence is important too. People ask why the effect of a sporting event like the Olympics doesn't last/have every child training for glory. Apart from the practicalities of expense, children see the distance between what they can do and the achievements of the athletes as too great. The gap is too wide and few children have the will to wait and undergo the long arduous training. Only a few can encompass the delayed gratification of succeeding many years down the line.

A further complexity arises because individual children all want to practise different things. They have different aspirations (although these may be subsumed in trying to please) and different temperaments that impinge on learning. Practitioners try to discern these in many different children through observing their competence in different environments and then planning appropriate learning opportunities. They then evaluate their plan in the light of what each child has learned (see Chapter 3). They have a mammoth task.

WHEN DOES LEARNING BEGIN?

Learning begins before birth. Pediatricians and mothers themselves have found that the baby in the womb quietens to listen to the rhythm of the mother's talk, or to her favourite music. The debate as to whether this constitutes learning goes on! Certainly the baby must be listening. The research on reflexes and their presence/timing of inhibition and their effects on future learning shows that the ideal learning process should flow seamlessly from conception on. In the womb strength develops over the nine months' gestation and as the foetus kicks and turns in the amniotic fluid, it is learning about body boundary, i.e. where it ends and the outside begins. This is elementary spatial awareness, a basic motor competence. The sense of balance, the vestibular sense, the first sense to be developed is working too to get the baby in the correct, head down position ready to be born. It is often called 'the leader of the sensory orchestra' because all other senses pass through it en route to the higher centres in the brain. It is fascinating to know that many breech births are caused by the vestibular sense not working well and that many of these children will have balance difficulties that can delay movement progress and hinder writing/motor skills later on. Understanding this can mean that practitioners can observe children's balance and prepare age related opportunities to promote it. Balance is part of everything children do. It is much more than being able to stand on one leg! So each action promotes balance – more so when it is done with care and attention as to how the different body parts contribute to the whole! 'Stand for a moment to get your balance' and 'gently on you go' are key instructions that should help eliminate rushing and falling.

THE MOTOR MILESTONES

The motor milestones give a rough guide as to when children should be able to sit and walk and run. The times given are general indicators of progress – e.g. some children will walk at 10 months, others at 18 months and both are fine, but any marked deviance from the norm has to be investigated without delay so that interventions to support the child can be put in place. The language milestones give guidance too. (See Appendices 1 and 2.)

SENSORY AWARENESS AND LEARNING

In this chapter reference has been made to the development of sensory perception and now the chapter gives indicators of possible sensory difficulties so that interventions to allay them may be put in place. Many practitioners will teach children about their senses, saying there are five. But there are more, even although these others would be too complex for most children to understand.

THE SENSES

See Table 2.2 for a summary of the senses.

TABLE 2.2 The senses

The senses	Their key role	Indicators of difficulties
Vestibular	Balance	Unsteadiness; unwilling to leave the ground or take risks, e.g. using a tricycle or climbing frame
Kinaesthetic	Spatial awareness	Unable to judge distances; bumping and spilling; knocking things over
Proprioceptive	Body awareness	General clumsiness; not knowing where the body parts are
Visual	Seeing and tracking	Squinting; rubbing eyes; holding a (functional sight) book too near or far from the face
Auditory	Listening and hearing	Distractibility; inability to focus
Tactile	Feeling and touching	Needs firm touch or can't bear to be touched; 'hyper' or 'hypo' reaction to pain and temperature
Taste and smell	Accept /reject food Judge distances	Unwilling to try foods Upset by strong smells

The vestibular sense

The first of the senses to be developed before birth is the vestibular sense, or sense of balance. It is situated in the inner ear with the auditory or hearing sense and is the leader of the sensory orchestra because all sensations must pass through the vestibular sense en route to the cerebral cortex, the thinking part of the brain. In the womb, the vestibular sense gets the baby the right way up to be born. Breech babies may have a poor sense of balance (because the vestibular sense was weak before birth) and a poor sense of hand dominance. After the birth, the vestibular sense helps children cope with gravity. A poor vestibular sense is present in dyslexia and dyspraxia.

Poor vestibular sense

The following list gives difficulties or observation points indicating a poor vestibular sense:

- a poor sense of balance;
- motion sickness;
- dislike of quick changes of direction;
- avoidance of equipment such as a climbing frame;
- being easily disoriented (hence, keep the environment calm and unflustered);
- bumping and dropping things;
- difficulty in staying still.

The kinaesthetic and proprioceptive senses

Although these two names are often used interchangeably, the kinaesthetic sense only comes into play when the body is moving, whereas the proprioceptive sense works all the time to relay positional information.

The proprioceptors are all over the body: in the skin, muscles and joints (receptors are even located in the hair follicles), and they literally tell us where we end and the outside world begins. So children with a poor proprioceptive sense often have difficulty in keeping still – they have to move so that their kinaesthetic and proprioceptive senses provide them with more secure information about where they are in space.

Poor kinaesthetic or proprioceptive sense

The following list gives difficulties or observation points indicating a poor kinaesthetic or proprioceptive sense:

- a poor sense of poise, e.g. the child who slumps over the table at craftwork or 'folds' when sitting on the floor at story time;
- easily tired by the constant effort needed to stay erect;
- constant movement and fidgeting (provide a beanbag to sit on and something to squeeze);
- poor depth perception, e.g. in misjudging the depth of stairs;
- poor sense of direction (rehearse 'where to go' ahead of the child having to do so independently);
- poor body awareness (play 'Simon says' types of games; for ideas see Macintyre (2003)).

The visual sense

Assessing vision should cover much more than reading/distance vision that is often the main concern in a simple eye test. Children who 'pass' this can still have difficulties in tracking, i.e. following the words on a page or the writing on the board. Functional vision depends on maturation of the central nervous system. Visual-motor integration skills are also very important: the two eyes have to work together to focus on an image (convergence). Some children with poor convergence see double images that confuse letter recognition; others will see the letters move on the page and may endure severe eye strain trying to adjust to the movement. This is known as Mears-Irlen syndrome and can be helped by coloured overlays or coloured lenses in spectacles. Children also benefit from being allowed to choose the colour of paper that suits them best, for different colours cut out light reflection.

Children must also be able to adjust their focus so that they can decipher objects and print from different angles and directions. This is called accommodation. The three skills – convergence, accommodation and tracking – are all prerequisites for quick identification and reading fluently without strain.

Poor visual sense

The following list gives difficulties or observation points indicating a poor visual sense:

- poor tracking skills;
- child saying that letters jump or overlap on the page;
- rubbing eyes or partially closing them to keep out the light;
- distress at being asked to choose a book.

The auditory sense

During the first three years, the child listens to and learns to tune in to sounds of their mother tongue. Thereafter, it is harder to adjust to the sounds of another language. Obviously, loss of hearing significantly affects learning, but children who 'can hear' may have auditory discrimination problems and these may be the basis of a recognised additional learning need, e.g. dyslexia or dyspraxia. If children cannot hear the difference between 'p' and 'b' or 'sh' and 'th', both reading and spelling will be impaired. Even silent reading is affected because children listen to an inner voice – if the sounds are not clear, this process will be affected in the same way as in reading aloud.

Hearing too much (i.e. auditory hypersensitivity) can cause as much difficulty as not hearing enough. Children bombarded by sound can have difficulty selecting what they need to hear from the variety of different noises around them. Even in a quiet classroom, some children find hearing the teacher difficult, as they cannot cut out minor rustles and squeaks.

Poor auditory sense

The following list gives difficulties or observation points indicating a poor auditory sense:

- oversensitive to sounds;
- confusion in distinguishing sounds;
- delay in responding;
- constantly asking for things to be repeated.

The tactile sense

Tactility or sensitivity to touch is important in feeding, in communicating and in generally feeling secure. Touch is one of the earliest sources of learning, and touch receptors cover the whole body. They are linked to a headband in the brain: the somatosensory cortex, which registers heat, cold, pressure, pain and body position. It makes an important contribution to the sense of balance.

Some children have a system that is overreactive to touch, and this causes them to be distressed by responses that most children welcome, such as hugs. This can make them isolated especially because families can mistakenly interpret their reactions as rejection. Yet these same children can be 'touchers' seeking out sensory stimulation through contacting others, even though they themselves would be distressed by such overtures.

Pain receptors can cause difficulties too. Some children are hyposensitive and may not feel pain or temperature change. They may tolerate holding hot plates or go out of doors without dressing for protection against icy winds. And the hypersensitive ones will overreact to injections and visits to the dentist because they feel so much pain. Some children feel pain even when having their nails or hair cut. All kinds of problems arise from being hypo- or hyper-touch-sensitive.

Poor tactile sense

The following list gives difficulties or observation points indicating a poor tactile sense:

- dislike of being touched, so withdrawing from contact;
- compulsively touching others;
- pain may cause over- or under-reaction;
- poor temperature control;
- allergies – possibly eczema;
- dislike of contact sports/games;
- if the child lacks protective control, he may not sense danger.

The senses of smell and touch

The sense of smell is the most evocative of the senses as it can stimulate memories, e.g. of a hot summer when the milk turned sour. The sense of smell can also stimulate the hormones controlling appetite, temperature and sexuality. Certain smells can become associated with different situations, e.g. the smell of a hospital can conjure up memories of pain, or the scent of flowers can recall a happy event such as a wedding, or a sad one such as a funeral.

The sense of taste depends on the sense of smell, so it is not difficult to understand why children refuse to accept new foods simply because they do not like the appearance or the smell. Some of the earliest learning comes through these senses; as we know, during the sensorimotor period, the baby will put everything to the mouth. This most sensitive part of the body will tell them about the taste and texture of the object and whether it is hard, soft or malleable, as well as whether the taste is pleasant or not.

Poor sense of taste and smell

The following list gives difficulties or observation points indicating a poor sense of taste or smell:

- children may be very fussy about new foods and only tolerate a very restricted diet;
- they may refuse to go to the bathroom because of the smell of antiseptics or even of scented soap;
- they may dislike being near other people especially if they wear perfume or aftershave.

SENSORY INTEGRATION

When children appear distressed it is vital to consider that their sensory input may be 'hyper' or 'hypo', i.e. giving too much input or too little. The child who bangs and crashes may not be receiving the signals that would allow him to cope in a gentler way. On the other hand, even a flickering light or a rustle may cause a sensitive child to be upset. Some children can explain what is wrong, but others, especially those on the autistic spectrum, will think you are already aware of their problems and fail to explain. Unfortunately, they may believe that nothing can be done. But practitioners can take steps so that the learning environment compensates for sensory difficulties.

Chapter 3

Observation, assessment, planning, intervention and evaluation

The OAPIE cycle

This chapter considers the cycle of observation, assessment, planning, intervention and evaluation (of the plan) that guides practitioners in their daily interactions with children in early years settings.

Practitioners understanding development and developing eyes that can identify changes in the children through careful observation is the cornerstone of education in the early years. The curriculum is child-centered, based on play, *the* key learning activity for young children. Through observation, practitioners ascertain the developmental status of each child in each aspect of development and plan learning opportunities to foster the skills and abilities they will need to cope with the vast amount of learning that lies ahead. The individuality of the children, the differences in their languages and cultural expectations and sometimes the input from parents who are naturally anxious about their child's development, but may have fixed views on 'what education should be about', can make this a fascinating, if daunting task.

Listen to some practitioners explain their successes and problems:

We have academically able children who need an extended curriculum; we have children with global developmental delay who need reinforcement and overlearning of the most basic things; some who want to participate in all the activities and some that won't join in at all. We have children with physical difficulties such as cerebral palsy that shouldn't be bumped and one or two children who only know how to barge. We have to support them all. We have to provide challenges for them all and recognise when they succeed. It's a wonderful job, but it's complex and in this culture of litigation, full of risks that we might inadvertently offend. This is a huge concern. Some days, on top of all this and especially when staff are ill or resources

FIGURE 3.1 Sam is investigating where birds nest

get vandalised or even when the weather's really bad and the children can't get outside to play, we are left asking, 'What can we do?'

Anna, a newly appointed teacher, explains her philosophy:

> We try to find a balance between being very open and friendly and supportive to each parent and child and establishing a routine that gives the children security and allows the staff to establish a curriculum that extends their interests and their learning. If we are to monitor the children's progress, we need to plan appropriate activities and organise the resources to allow us to do this. We also want to share our findings with the parents and find if they are happy with how their child is doing or if we should be adjusting our curriculum in any way. Most parents understand how complex this is and they are ready to co-operate and make suggestions and contributions. They give us positive feedback most of the time. But some parents seem to think that nursery is only free childminding so we have to set 'rules' e.g. we tell them, 'Your children do best when they arrive at the correct time, wide awake, ready to enjoy the nursery routine.' Although we understand the extreme difficulties some parents face and we wonder how we would cope, we have to establish ground rules too. We understand 'legitimate reasons' and we can provide breakfast snacks or extra scarves and gloves. None of that is a problem, but frustration

builds up when 3-year-olds tell us, 'We were skiving off yesterday. We slept in and then watched the telly.' And they do!

Practitioners just at the start of their careers have many more day-to-day questions about doing their job. Ruby, a first-year nursery nurse student on placement, explains:

> I am supposed to be observing a small group of children and looking out over the others but they rush around all the time. I try to find out what they are doing but they won't wait. I just don't know what to write down. I made some notes yesterday saying Max knew his colours and I thought I'd better check it out today. He got them all wrong and rushed off to play in the water. My other notes are just rubbish. What am I going to say at today's staff meeting? I don't seem to have noticed anything useful at all.

I should think that all early years staff could sympathise with Ruby. She is finding observation is a skill that is acquired slowly, especially when children, as she says, 'won't wait'. Perhaps, as a starter, she could make a chart and ask the more experienced members of staff to give her ideas about specific things to observe. Then, when she gains confidence and greater insight into the particular child being observed, she can take a more open-ended stance and record what she sees, knowing it will be useful. At first recording details can seem a bit tedious, but it is only when a number of observations come together (e.g. in another area Max may have spoken about a blue truck or a red bus and another member of staff could then confirm that he does know his colours) that assessments can come alive and contribute to a profile of the child's development.

Nursery nurse Jason has been four years in the same setting and has built sound relationships with the families who come to the nursery, yet there are still issues that perplex him and cause him to reflect and ask the question 'why?'. In this instance he explains,

> I have three children from the same family in my nursery. The two boys appear confident and carefree while the little girl, Ali, the youngest one is withdrawn and shy. When she came with Mum and the boys to nursery and went home again, she seemed quite interested in what was going on. But now that she has the chance to stay, she won't. Every day she cries and wants to go home.

None of us anticipated this and Mum wants to go back to work. She seems to be blaming us and she tells us that her job can't be interrupted by calls. What can we do?

Ali is probably sensing that Mum needs to get away and she is feeling insecure. She won't know Mum's workplace and so her worries overwhelm the advantages of being familiar with the nursery. It is difficult to anticipate how children will react when asked to spend time apart from their parents; and the fact that her brothers settled easily won't really help, especially if Mum makes comparisons in Ali's hearing. Perhaps there is a quiet corner where she could play with just one or two caring children? Once she can establish a secure space and a friend, she might become more confident. But the main thing is to have patience, and in the meantime to try to distract her – possibly by giving her a special task, e.g. setting out a snack, or making a necklace for her Mum. This can be added to by giving her some gentle, and possibly private, positive feedback.

Connor is a special needs assistant with responsibility for Jay, a 5-year-old with Asperger's syndrome, and also needs to spend some time with the other children. Jay is very bright, but because of Jay's difficulties in interacting with other children, Connor is fascinated to learn how children develop social skills and how poor communication hinders learning. He has found it difficult to enhance the social skills of Tim, a 4-year-old for whom he is also responsible. Tim's parents have not alerted the nursery to any problem. Connor asks,

How can I get children to make the move from playing alone to playing together? I understand Jay's social difficulties and I am working on helping him to recognise the feelings that come over in facial expressions. But I'm not sure how to support Tim. He is very solitary. He is happy if he is left to play alone, but even when we sit on the carpet for story he moves away from the child beside him, no matter who it is. He reacts angrily, punching and spitting if we try to shift him. It would help him if he could be more relaxed and sociable before he goes to the next class. How can we help him?

Tim is obviously a very unhappy, insecure little boy. Helping him to tolerate other children is not easy and needs infinite patience. Connor could try thinking of ways to gradually reduce the space between Tim and another child, e.g. giving him a beanbag to sit on at story time and very gradually moving that nearer a child on another beanbag might work, because the beanbag might mark 'his space' and help him feel secure. But this will take time.

It might be helpful to find the activity that Tim enjoys best and then find someone with the same interests to share the activity with him. It is the activity rather than the person that is important. Tim enjoys building pathways in the sand, but gives up his game when other boys or girls approach. Perhaps he is afraid that tossed sand will get in his eyes. Perhaps, like Jay, he is recognising his social difficulties, for example, not being able to read the non-verbal communication of other children and so not being able to respond appropriately. Allowing him to stay at the sand alone and then with just one other quiet child, e.g. gentle, easy-going Max, is worth a try, especially if he knows the other children are busy with other activities and won't intrude. If that worked, then perhaps Mum could ask that child home, so that building up a friendship is possible. Would Tim allow Max to play nearby? As he has Asperger's, he wouldn't make any social demands yet they each would sense the other was there.

It is also important to find out if Tim's parents find his solitariness an issue at home. Perhaps they are loners too and don't see the need for social interaction. Perhaps they have very different ideas about what is best for Tim.

Of course, suggesting things to parents can be hard, as they may interpret ideas or strategies to help as a criticism of the way they are bringing up their child. It is even trickier if parents' views and the early years setting's views on what is best for the child conflict. Emily, a very experienced early years teacher, tells of such an issue. She explains:

> Lee is a great child and can happily paint and do craft and bake – he enjoys everything we have to offer. But his Mum wants him to learn to read and write and when she brings him to nursery she always leaves him with 'Go and find a book now . . . or do your writing'. I tried to explain that formally teaching reading and writing isn't really part of our curriculum, that he'll do that at the next stage. But some children, particularly the girls, I find enjoy fine motor skills like writing so we do provide opportunities for emergent writing but we would never force a child because they all develop control at different times. We have lots of books and we encourage all the children to browse and explain what they see in the pictures and every day they join in storytelling.

Lee's Mum is anxious, as many parents are, because they do not appreciate the vast amount of learning that precedes more formal education

FIGURE 3.2 Lee and Eli practise emergent writing. Lee doesn't find writing much fun!

FIGURE 3.3 Every day children enjoy stories, learn descriptive words and come to understand the sequence of events

and how this is all covered in the early years, play-based curriculum. Perhaps at a parents' evening this could be explained or instances of opportunities for word recognition and emergent writing/number could be pointed out? Some early years settings have a leaflet for parents to study at home, but sometimes this isn't enough. Practitioners have always to remember that some parents might also have difficulties reading English. If parents request more detail, perhaps the early years setting could invest in a book to lend, e.g. 'Planning the pre-5 setting' (see Macintyre and McVitty (2003) for details). Then the parents will be sure that their children are not 'just playing' and this will allow them to recognise the stress-free learning that develops as children play.

Perhaps even more delicate and challenging is knowing what best to say and do when a child experiences bereavement for the first time. Dave was shattered to find he had no words to comfort Rachael, whose grandpa had died. Moreover, he was unsure of the faith status of the little girl or the family and, in the light of the health and safety policy, was unable to offer a hug in place of words. He explains:

> Rachael rushed up to me and said, 'Grandpa's gone.' I didn't know what had happened so I asked, 'Gone where?' The tears welled up so I knew and felt absolutely dreadful. 'I don't know,' Rachael whispered, but then she smiled and added, 'but he'll come back when he's better, won't he?' What could I say?

And what is the best way forward when staff suspect a child may have an additional learning need, and parents deny that this is the case? This happened to Maria. She explains:

> We have this little boy Omar, who is 14 months. He is very floppy and makes no attempt to pull himself up to standing even when he is wanting out of his cot. He is sitting unsupported for very brief spells but soon topples over. His Mum says she has taken him to their GP and has been told there is nothing wrong. In the nursery we are unsure whether there is something really wrong or whether he will get stronger as he matures. He is always first into nursery at 8 a.m. and last to be picked up at 6 in the evening. What happens in between we don't know, but we suspect he's put to bed with not much stimulation? What should we do?

These cases are tricky. The parents have to agree to contact being made with the health visitor, who would be the key person for a child of this age. The cut-off point between delayed development (where hopefully the child will catch up once he matures and gets stronger) and the signs of a syndrome (such as dyspraxia, for example, where early intervention is essential) is not clearly defined. If the parents do not wish the nursery to contact the health visitor and concerns continue, then building up a friendly relationship with the parent(s) is the best way. Giving positive feedback (e.g. 'Omar stretched out and held his car for quite a time and chortled with happiness today') may help them relax and see that you would like to build a partnership to support their child. They may be very unhappy about the child's progress but could be at the stage of denying that anything is amiss. Pointing out positive things is a subtle way of indicating the level of what is being achieved – but this strategy needs time, patience and tact. On the other hand, Omar's Mum might feel inadequate and believe that the early years environment is better then the one she can provide at home. Eventually, if staff consider that the child is being harmed by non-action, then the early years or school head teacher would decide the next steps. No early years practitioner should act alone.

UNDERSTANDING DEVELOPMENT AND DEVELOPING OBSERVATION SKILLS ARE KEY PROCESSES IN EARLY YEARS SETTINGS

This is because education in the early years settings is child-centred. This means that the staff observe the children carefully, and monitor and record what they do in each aspect of their development – social, emotional, intellectual, moral and motor. The information is recorded, dated and discussed so that a full and accurate profile of each child's progress is built up over time. The observations also pinpoint what teaching input each child requires and so can be used in planning the programme of opportunities and experiences that will promote each child's learning. They also identify particular strengths so that staff can prepare extension work. This may be in the form of resources, e.g. a book that matches the child's interests or craft materials that enable the child to complete a piece of work to a high level. Observations can also highlight any difficulties that need special intervention, e.g. if a child was finding it difficult to cross the midline of the body, then the ability to crawl would be checked, for this competence is needed to develop cross-lateral co-ordination. It is very important that individual gifts and talents across the developmental spectrum are fostered, and that needs are identified, monitored and, hopefully, alleviated, possibly even before the child knows they are there.

OBSERVING AND RECORDING

It takes time to master the skill of observing children, i.e. to develop eyes that can spot individual differences. This is because there is just so much to see and rarely will the children sit and wait while practitioners check their recordings. They are usually anxious to get on with the business of playing, not really aware that observers might be left behind. This is why practitioners often feel overwhelmed by recording examples of behaviour that can build into a useful profile of a child's progress. However, when they see how different recordings (always named and dated) come together, they can be convinced that their own detail is valuable in compiling a meaningful picture. Sometimes, experienced and new observers may see different things when they observe the same child, but this can add to the richness of discussion. Having the observer's name added to the recording can also show the range of things each observer sees. The best plan is to video the children, especially when these discrepancies occur, for then the tape can be replayed and paused at relevant points, giving observers time to review their observations, possibly from a different perspective. Having a video also lets absent staff or parents share specially interesting moments of progress.

Sometimes staff can be asked to observe a specific competence, e.g. 'Time on task' as a means of gathering evidence to ascertain a child's attention span, or whether the children were limiting learning by being too attached to one area or one toy. In that case staff might be asked: 'Record how long Sharon stays at each activity and note what she chooses to do.' This time-sampling method would limit what was to be noted. This observation is not asking for quality, i.e. how well Sharon does or what language she uses when she interacts with other children. Only a time-frame is required. Noting the purpose of the observation is useful as a reference for later reflection on progress (see Table 3.1).

This observation, combined with a number of others, confirms the practitioner's fears that Sharon's behaviour is bordering on being obsessive, so the staff discuss what to do. Should they hide the pram? Would this force Sharon to choose something else or would it take away her security? Should they ignore the behaviour hoping that other interests will take over as Sharon becomes more confident in the early years setting? Answers to questions like this depend on knowing the child well and anticipating her reactions. This is what makes planning based on observations so time-consuming and difficult, but so vitally important.

A second example concerns Sean. Staff are gathering evidence to show how his aggressive behaviour is affecting his social skills (see Table 1.2).

TABLE 3.1 Time sampling (1)

Planned time: every 3 minutes	*Child*: Sharon. *Observer*: Leanne Observation to find time spent on one activity. Query obsession.
13.00	Searches for pram, grabs the handle and wanders round the outside of the room. She doesn't check if the doll is inside. She is rocking the pram fiercely and watching the wheels spin.
13.03	Sally asks for the pram. Sharon glares and tries to push the pram into her – Sally retreats, putting out her tongue.
13.06	Jackie approaches and they go to the house area together, Sharon is still gripping the pram. She struggles to get it inside, ignoring pleas to 'Leave it at the door'.
13.09	They settle there. Sharon tries to close the door.
13.12	They have made a tea party. She still holds the pram.
13.15	Jackie asks if the doll wants tea. Sharon shakes her head. She has never looked for the doll. The pram is the important thing.
13.20	Jackie has fetched a different doll. The tea party resumes.

TABLE 3.2 Time sampling (2)

Name:	Sean aged 4.8 (second year in nursery). Observation: no. 8 this term
Time	Observed activity
9.00	Races into room, throws coat into corner and won't say 'Good morning'.
9.01	Turns and hits another boy, then heads for the large construction area where he dismantles a 'castle', knocking the bricks roughly to the floor.
9. 05	Sits beside the teacher facing the group to sing 'Good Morning to everyone' jingle. Scowls when asked to join the others.
9.07	Can't relax – shoulders very tense. Asks: 'When can I get the bricks?'
9.08	Teacher asks him to sit quietly for a moment more. He struggles up and runs across the room. He bangs into a table and yells out about his sore leg.
9.10	He has found his coat and yells out, 'I'll tell my mother on you.'

A ten-minute observation like this details reactions and attitudes. It provides evidence of Sean's anxiety and would be collated with other recordings so that an emotional profile could be produced for a psychologist should there be need for expert support.

Another observation might concern movement skills. In this case, the competences to be observed are set out and there is a three-day time scale (see Table 3.3).

However, there are times when staff are given one child or a small group to observe and they are asked to 'record what you see', often on sticky labels that can later be put together in a file. These then form the basis of discussions with more and less experienced practitioners all making contributions.

TABLE 3.3 Example of three-day observation

Name: Janna Date: 14.10.13–17.10.13 Observer: Helen	Yes, can do	No, cannot do
Can crawl		*
Can stand and sit still	*	
Can pick up small objects using the pincer grip		*
Can hold a paintbrush comfortably	*	
Can climb on the frame		*
Can cope independently at the toilet		*
Can balance on a wide bench	*	
Can control a pencil		*

18-10-13

Martin is confident on the climbing frame. He can explain what he wants to do and knows 'I can jump higher than anyone else in the nursery.'

Aim: To set out a difficult challenge with ropes and hurdles and see if he can negotiate that and self-evaluate his performance.

FIGURE 3.4 Sticky label recording

One practitioner, Elise, did her time sampling through drawing a clock face and marking it into minute segments for a fifteen-minute observation. She was anxious to find out exactly what John did as he played on the large apparatus outdoors. She suspected that his balance was poor and she wanted to find how this affected his outdoor play. So she aimed to bring in both quantity (how often John did something) and quality (how successful he was). This was repeated three times then a summary was recorded. The key conclusions were:

- John was happy running in and out of the equipment outside and he enjoyed ground level activities e.g. pulling himself through the tunnels. However, his running action was floppy, showing poor leg strength.
- John avoided any climbing activity. He stood at the foot of the frame but made no attempt to climb.
- He tried to throw the large balls to a friend but the whole body action caused him to fall over.
- When he tried to run and jump over a small cushion he went so fast that he lost control and fell headlong into the grass.

At discussion time the team decided to focus on John's leg strength hoping that this would help his balance (see Figure 3.5).

Observation, assessment, planning and evaluating the plan in light of the child's responses are key processes in early years settings. Gathering observations is the first step towards making plans to provide the most appropriate teaching. This process can be seen as a cycle (see Figure 3.6).

This schedule has a part for recording the efficacy of the intervention that was tried. This allows a greater width of discussion and saves a second practitioner unaware of the first intervention trying the same and so wasting time and effort. Sometimes words used interchangeably can cause confusion. It is best if 'assessment' is kept for the child's progress or regression and 'evaluation' for looking critically at the plan.

Table 3.4 shows two plan examples.

Activity to help develop body awareness: observations leading to OAPIE cycle

One favourite rhyme practised in many if not most early years settings is 'Head, shoulders, knees and toes' and once these easily recognised parts are known then the jingle can be extended to bring in other parts and

FIGURE 3.5 John playing

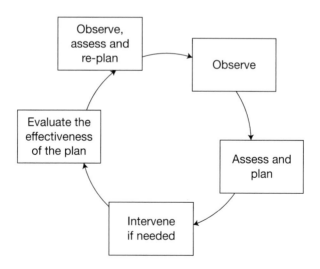

FIGURE 3.6 The OAPIE cycle

TABLE 3.4 Example plans

Name: Rory B. Age 18 months	Date of Observation. 16.5.12	Plan 1 – teach crawling Plan 2 – strengthen muscles	Assessment / Action	Evaluation
Note: Sitting unsupported achieved.	Poor muscle tone preventing crawling.	Encourage lying on front pushing up; pull bent legs in to hold flat back table position. Share stages of crawling with Mum and ensure she knows cross lateral pattern.	Initially R. resented being on front but dangling a balloon encouraged him to look up then press up with arms. Flops down. Try rolling over from back to front and pushing up.	Some strengthening of arms – legs still floppy. Encourage pushing feet against P. hand to give resistance – also splashing in water to help awareness.
Name: Ria S. Age 36 months	Date of Observation. 19.6.12	Plan 1 – Check vocabulary / comprehension Plan 2 – Record conversation	Assessment / Action	Evaluation
	Ria has an outstanding vocabulary but other children do not understand – communica- tion is one sided. She retreats and 'reads' her favourite books.	Listen carefully to find if language is appropriate. Use turn taking games e.g. rolling a ball to a partner to encourage waiting for a response	Language was appropriate but very fast. Difficult to hold her attention. Very frustrated.	Change to recording on tape and listening to her own speech. Ask her to talk to a baby doll and explain speed differences.

'challenges.' So beginning with the well known verses (Not my work but repeated here in case they are not known), add the next two and extend the jingles to make others.

Heads, shoulders, knees and toes, knees and toes,
Heads, shoulders, knees and toes, knees and toes,
Eyes and ears and chin and nose,
Heads, shoulders, knees and toes. Knees and toes.

Heads, shoulders, knees and toes, knees and toes,
Heels, bottoms, backs and nose, backs and nose,
Tap your shoulders, turn right round,
Reach for the sky then touch the ground, touch the ground.

Make your fingers stretch out wide, stretch out wide.
Clap your hands against your side your side,
Make them whirl you round and round, then
Sit very quietly on the ground, on the ground.

(verses 2 and 3 written by Christine Macintyre)

What new learning/movement challenge is implicit in these extra verses?

In verse 2, the children tap their heels, their bottoms and their backs. These body parts are not mentioned so often in activities and some children find it difficult to know where they are. Tapping 'behind' also adds a balance challenge. Developing this awareness also helps getting dressed and wiping at the toilet. A useful observation is whether children can recognise and then tap parts of their bodies that are difficult to see. If this is difficult then having children in twos, each pointing out the parts on each other's bodies can be a fun lead in.

In verse 3, 'Tap your shoulders' should mean that the arms cross to tap on the other side of the body. This provides a good 'crossing the midline' observation and backs up observations linked to the inability to crawl using the cross lateral pattern/retention of the ATNR reflex.

Examples of observations and interventions

One child, Amelie, who could not cope with this was observed by practitioner Laura. Her recordings and subsequent plan are shown in Table 3.5.

Amelie was confused in this activity. She was very unsure where her body parts were and she was baffled by the speed of the jingle. Using

TABLE 3.5 The OAPIE cycle in action

| Name:
Amelie
Age
3 years
4 months | Date of
Observation:
12.8.13
Activity
Head,
shoulders
knees and
toes with
extension
verses. | Plan A – Develop
body awareness
to reduce
clumsiness.
Slow pace of
jingle to ensure
balance is OK.
Plan B –
Increase focus
on hands. | Assessment/
Action
A. very slow
to respond in
rhyme.
Hands lack
control –
won't attempt
to cross the
midline. | Evaluation
Begin simpler
hand
awareness
activities –
check hand
dominance.
Use throwing
bean bags into
a pail and
balancing
beanbags on
head/back of
hands.
N.B. Check
development of
pincer grip. |
| 10.9.13 | Activity
1) Drawing
round fingers
to focus
attention.
2) Drawing
round body
then naming
body parts.
3) Recapping
first verse of
H, S, K and
T. | 1) Poorly
developed pincer
grip made this
impossible.
2) A. enjoyed this
and was able to
say where several
body parts were. | 1) Draw
patterns in
wet sand.
2) Bury small
toys from
child's world
game in sand.
A. has to
retrieve them.
This provides
resistance/
strengthens
fingers. | Now try songs
with pointing
to isolate
different
fingers e.g.
Peter pointer.
2) Work with
a doll to talk
about elbows
and ankles,
heels and
knees.
3) A. now able
to join in H, S,
K and T verse
1 repeated
building up
speed. |

this activity as a model, observations led to assessments, interventions and evaluations.

Earlier in the chapter Elise had been concerned about John's poor balance/leg strength. Given the evidence on her time sampling record, her line manager decided to share their concerns with John's parents and if agreeable the setting would try to obtain physiotherapy help. In the meantime they planned activities such as marching in groups. They hoped that beating the ground would provide resistance and so strengthen John's legs. The 'Marching like soldiers' would encourage good posture and strength throughout the body while 'Halt' would be a fun way of gaining control. The practitioners set out the OAPIE framework (see Table 3.6).

At first the team was disappointed that little improvement was obvious, however the physiotherapists found the record helpful as a starting point for their work. They carried on with posture activities and took John swimming so that he could try balance activities while being supported by the water. They assured the team that their intervention was useful for John and that he had told them what a strong soldier he was. He had gained confidence in his posture; his gait had improved.

So the time sampling method records what children choose to do and where necessary can provide evidence of obsessive behaviour, physical inability or simply a tentative attitude towards trying anything new. Some children need time to stand back and watch others and knowing they are supposed to be busy they may make ineffectual actions just to cover up the fact that they need this watching time. They may be deliberating how to get involved or be considering alternative strategies. The time sampling could clarify whether this was a passing phase or indicate that a learning difficulty was emerging. This method could then pinpoint issues for further study.

TABLE 3.6 An OAPIE plan for John

Name: John Age: 4 years	Observation	Assessment	Plan	Evaluation of plan.
	John avoids climbing – stays with activities at ground level. Move too fast and loses control.	Poor balance, leg strength?	In groups of 4, play Marching, Halt turning corners with control. Give warning of change e.g. Ready? Halt! Plan 2 Try Giant soldiers that make a lot of noise stamping into the ground.	Seemed to enjoy 'soldiers' but didn't put much effort into action. Much more effort but tipped over – change Giants back to soldiers now the idea is grasped. This should encourage better posture.

Chapter 4

Play – a child's life

Play is the foundation stone of the early years curriculum yet it is hard to encompass all the good things in one succinct definition. Practitioners appreciating how all aspects of development are nurtured in play will sympathise and very probably agree with a colleague who, asked to define play, replied, 'Trying to define play is like trying to catch the wind in a paper bag.' She was envisaging the myriad of unexpected and creative happenings that can be observed in different play scenarios and denying that one definition could do justice to them all! However parents and inspectors demand a more tangible explanation which explains what the essence of the play curriculum is. A very considered and lovely definition was written by Susan Isaacs in 1933. It has stood the test of time. She wrote,

> Play is a child's life and the means by which he comes to understand the world around him.

She was explaining that children develop knowledge and understandings about themselves and their environment through play. Play is their work. In the earliest days children's development is usually applauded and surrounded by smiles and admiration but little children are self-centered too. They are quite insular beings, as yet unable to make many responses. While this may be less gratifying for families, it also means that any early days difficulty such as postnatal depression does not spoil bonding. There is time for this to happen for bonding is a process that develops over time rather than an instant attachment – at least on the part of the baby (Robinson 2011). Moreover, the children develop at their own speed, without anyone telling them what to do or how to make things better! They can make choices about what to do and when to stop doing it. They do not have to worry about failing to meet some standard set by someone else. Isn't it a pity that this time is so short?

Isaacs observed play/interactions from the first weeks of the baby's life when they were just able to respond to overtures that encouraged bonding and attachment. This would involve turning their heads and holding eye contact, gradually learning to smile and holding their arms out to be cuddled. (Cephalo-caudal and proximo distal development can be observed when this happens.) Then at four months or so, the children play with their hands, often described as their first toy. This develops hand awareness and the ability to work at and cross the midline of the body, an important basis for more sophisticated coordinated movements such as fastening buttons and carrying out many of the activities of daily living later on. And when parents and/or practitioners dangle a toy to encourage stretching and grasping, they are also promoting spatial awareness and dexterity. It is fascinating to watch as babies' movements gradually change from being wavering and 'clumsy' to becoming accurate and efficient. This demonstrates the inborn natural progression due to maturation/nature being complemented by interaction with an adult who understands the value of playing and through this provides appropriate nurture.

As babies learn to sit, their arms are freed to participate in games such as peek-a-boo. Apart from being enjoyable, the game teaches turn taking (a precursor to language development) and 'object constancy' i.e. the baby gradually realises that when Mum 'disappears' for a moment behind the cloth, she is still there. This is an important developmental milestone. If however babies are not interested or even upset by such early games then they can switch off, often leaving the adult bereft. The baby is in charge so the best way is to wait and try again later. The baby may not be at the stage of readiness that makes games like this pleasurable. This is an opportunity for observation, assessment, planning and evaluation. Adults sensibly decide that no intervention is needed, it is best to wait. But this is a considered decision based on knowledge of age related competence and each particular child, not a laissez-faire attitude that results in doing nothing! Isn't it interesting that even in the first months, the baby stays in control?

Fundamentally, this is why the early years curriculum is child-centered, based on play. For in play the children can experiment and do things that may never have occurred to adults. They can develop their creativity and engage in problem solving without fear of failing to meet some preset goal. They also have the freedom to wander off and try out other activities. They learn from others in their peer group who are likely to be playing at a similar developmental level and therefore doing things they might like to try too. They learn from absorbing ideas and so extend their thinking without an adult intervening and even spoiling their game. Very often it takes courage for practitioners to stay back and observe. They feel they must intervene because they feel conditioned to be busy.

Play develops in a sequence linked to the developing maturational competences the children display. As they become less tied to the here and now, they begin to imagine events that might happen and at three years of age memories begin to take root and stay with them acting as the basis of further decision making and learning. It is difficult for anyone to remember things that happened before age three. Can you?

Sometimes parents must be helped to widen their understanding of what constitutes play. In the earliest times, when children engage in sensory motor play, they are experimenting to discover the properties of objects in the environment. Through mouthing, they discover the taste, texture and malleability of different things. They are thinking and problem-solving, often designing ways to tantalise adults e.g. in emptying cupboards – but these experiences help them move through the developmental stages of play. The children are 'asking' a whole range of questions, e.g. How do I do this? Where does that go? If I drop this biscuit over the side of the table, will it come back? Will anyone be annoyed? If Mummy goes out of the room, does she disappear? How can I follow her?

SENSORIMOTOR PLAY

Very young children, up to about 12 months or so, discover the properties of objects (i.e. their hardness, softness, malleability, their taste and smell), by feeling and tasting, and studying how they move. The high level of sensory input gives this type of play its name. The children also learn to pass objects from hand to hand across the midline of the body, developing their hand dominance and manipulative skills. And, as they reach and grasp, they are learning about distance and direction, i.e. how far the toy is away and how they have to adjust their position to reach it. Letting go is very difficult at this stage, but many important motor skills are being tried out as the children play.

CONSTRUCTIVE PLAY

Manipulating one object gradually leads to 2-year-olds experimenting with constructing things, e.g. building blocks, slotting parts of a puzzle

▨ TABLE 4.1 The changing patterns of play

Type of play	Age	Characteristics
Sensori-motor: early discovery about shape, texture, weight, taste, hardness, malleability	0–2 Solitary play	Exploration and perception Child discovering the properties of objects
Symbolic play: first signs of imagination/pretending	2–4 Parallel play, i.e. playing near another child without cooperating and with minimal interaction	Using one object to represent another, e.g. a yo-yo as a pet dog; a clothes peg as a doll
Simple construction: early recognition of patterns and tessellation	3+ Creating something with a friend: brief interactions soon abandoned. Children beginning to empathise with children with additional needs	Building towers (three blocks high) Enjoys stories, especially with repetition, e.g. the Little Red Hen
Pretend play: role play in context. Fantasy play becoming important	4+ Sustained play with a friend. Some small group interaction	Action songs enjoyed as balance and coordination improve Wider life experience allows taking roles of nurses, firemen, space games
Games with rules: football, chess, etc. Can make up rules for games	6+ Children begin to identify leaders and followers Play mainly in same-sex groups	Supporting teams; collecting team memorabilia

Source: Macintyre and McVitty (2003)

together, making something with clay. They handle both large and small objects with increasing dexterity as they develop the pincer grip, turning the pages of books and threading beads. But they mainly identify objects as they really are and use them for their recognised purpose rather than imagining they are something else. Some children have to be taught how to pretend and develop their life skills into pretence, e.g. 'brush your hair, now brush the dolly's hair' is a good way to begin. This is because the children can see these things happening – they are concrete experiences that don't demand too large an imaginative leap.

PRETEND PLAY

First phase

Pretend play develops further in the second year, but the children will still use a spoon to feed a doll, or pretend to give a doll a bath, or build bricks in the back of a truck. Although there is a burgeoning element of pretence in that the child may have imagined the doll was dirty or that the blocks were to be used to build a house, the objects are still used for their recognised function and the activities are those that the children have experienced themselves. The children are still tied up in their own perceptions of their world; they still analyse experiences in terms of what has happened to them.

Second phase

Between the ages of 2 and 3 years children begin to use symbols. This is an important development in the use of their imaginations. They discover that any object can be used as something else, e.g. a cardboard box can be a bus, with the child loudly ascertaining the imagined object is the real one. By the ages of 3 and 4 years this is the most common type of play.

Third phase: socio-dramatic play

This stage extends imaginative play and social interaction possibilities because children play together to act out a scene. The children depend on their mutual understandings about the roles of the doctor, nurse or bus driver, because these ideas drive the development of the play.

Being involved in shared ploys such as these can allow children to understand a different range of experiences and develop their imaginations too. They may never have been to hospital themselves, but following the lead of another child who has, they will soon don a doctor's coat and confidently apply a bandage or wield a stethoscope. Children learn much from their peer group because the things they copy are usually near their levels of understanding and skill. Adults' suggestions can often be far removed from their own thoughts.

This is the era of the 'imaginary friend'. Imaginary they may be, but they are real to the children who set places at table for them and become distressed if the friend gets 'lost'. Perhaps this is a way to develop empathy and altruism – an imaginary friend is sure to respond to overtures in an acceptable way? Or perhaps a friend who instinctively knows what you mean and doesn't make demands is more comforting than one who voices opinions and expects to share treats? For whatever reason, the imaginary friend is a normal part of childhood and is not a sign of a disturbed or a needy child. This phase will pass when other friendships develop.

RESOURCES TO DEVELOP CHILDREN'S IMAGINATIONS

In recent years early years settings have provided more brightly coloured resources than ever before, but to me many of them dictate the play rather than letting the children think of ideas for themselves. Children bake at a cooker, supplied with pots and spoons, or they dance with tutus – but they don't seem to fly to the moon on cardboard boxes any more.

Perhaps arranging a group of objects that together don't suggest any particular game could stimulate children to imagine something novel, or perhaps children could explain a game, then plan to resource it?

THE PROGRESSIONS IN PLAY ARE LINKED TO DEVELOPMENTS IN LANGUAGE AND MOVEMENT

Certainly, as muscle strength develops, children are enabled to do more things. This applies to both fine and gross motor skills. They need to develop control of the soft palate, lips and tongue before they can articulate words clearly; and once they can do this, they are able to express their intentions and wishes in play situations. Every action requires a level of co-ordination, which comes from muscle control. Table 4.2 is an attempt to link aspects of development in a time-frame. However, some children will travel at unequal speeds and some will have a more uneven pattern of development than others.

And as they do – or decide not to do – different play activities, adults observe and compare the children's progress and make difficult decisions about whether to intervene (if in doubt stay out!) and what to do. Achieving a balance between totally child-led play and adult initiated teaching is always a tricky problem. For there are things children need to learn to do and say and some skills e.g. learning colours, using the tripod grip to

TABLE 4.2 Aspects of development

	Play	Language	Movement
5 years	Can initiate or join in complex role-play.	Can follow a story without pictures. Can read simple words.	Can run and jump, ride a bike and zip a coat. Understands the rules of major games.
4 years	Understands pretence and develops fears of the unknown. Develops imaginative games, not always able to explain 'rules'.	Knows colours and numbers. Can explain events, hopes and disappointments.	Can climb and swing on large apparatus. Has a developed sense of safety outdoors. Can swim.
3 years	Enjoys group activities, e.g. baking a cake for someone's birthday. Understands turn-taking.	Uses complex sentences. Understands directional words and simple comparisons, e.g. big/small; long/short.	Can ride a trike; climb stairs with one foot to a step. Climbs in and out of car or bus without help.
2.5 years	Develops altruism especially for family members. Understands words such as 'sad', 'happy'.	Uses pronouns and past tenses. Adds 'ed' to form own version of past tense.	Uses a step-together pattern to climb stairs. Can walk some distance.
2 years	Beginning to play alongside and with a friend for a short time.	Rebels. States 'no'. Can form two-word sentences but comprehension far ahead of speech.	Still likes to be carried at times but can walk well. Jumping is difficult.
18 months	Sensorimotor play: children explore the properties of objects.	Children have vocabulary of 10 naming-words. Points to make wishes known.	Can crawl and walk but can't run or jump. Limbs are strong but balance can be precarious.

hold a paintbrush or pencil, knowing which hand/foot to use, can be taught when the time is right.

Leah was 4 years 3 months when this picture was taken. She was due to go to big school and the practitioners in the setting were concerned that she lacked hand dominance, i.e. she wasn't sure which hand to use. So they devised a game to help her. She was asked to crawl over from the corner, pick up a beanbag and throw it in the pail. After a few attempts

FIGURE 4.1 Leah is finding which hand gets the best score, so establishing a sense of hand dominance. Observe her floppy wrist and the effort shown by her protruding tongue. Perhaps this general lack of strength explains her delay in achieving hand dominance

she was asked, 'Which hand scores most points?' It happened to be her right hand and she was encouraged to have some more tries and count the number of points she scored. Later, when Leah looked hesitant before picking up a paintbrush, the staff were able to indicate her right hand and she smiled and complied. Gradually the confusion disappeared.

In Figure 4.1 Leah's general lack of strength is evident. She also uses a great deal of strength to throw the beanbag (look how her tongue protrudes with the effort she makes), so a general strengthening programme was also put in place.

The important step is to recognise 'readiness' and 'interest' and in many cases to pull back and wait, to trust that the children will develop the necessary competences to progress. This can be very hard for practitioners who have aims and targets in mind and possibly parents who do not realise that if children are overwhelmed by inappropriate input they will either rote learn or even withdraw from learning altogether. But when the waiting time is up and children's development is not matching the developmental milestones, then a more formal intervention needs to happen. Hopefully this can be in the form of a game where the child can be successful.

So, in play, children can

- Make choices about what they would like to do and where this should happen.
- Continue for a time and then abandon whatever they have chosen to do with no fear of failure or blame. They can go off to try something else.
- Practise the skills of daily living in a miniature safe way.
- Pretend to be someone else and develop understanding of different characters
- Make up a storyline and develop it to their own satisfaction
- Play alone or with a friend or in a group as they wish.

There is no time pressure to complete anything, no *necessary* end product although wonderful things do emerge (see Figure 4.2, Sam's dragon).

Children learn from others in their peer group too because they are likely to be sharing a similar level of development so that their skills are within the grasp of the playing child.

N.B. When children are playing, observation can happen in a natural unforced way so decisions about intervention can be valid, free from the pressure and tension that causes recordings to be biased.

FIGURE 4.2 Sam's delight in his dragon reveals the physical skills and intellectual learning (imagination, creativity, problem-solving) necessary to produce this artifact. He has selected materials and designed the dragon without anyone telling him to stop and move on to something else or even suggesting how to do it better. The ownership remains with him. This is very different from being told, 'Today everyone will make a dragon. Use pieces of card of the same length!' The quality of the interaction is very different.

IS PLAY ALWAYS FUN?

So is play always fun? Of course not. Some children are overwhelmed by the freedom play offers. They prefer to be told what to do. This may be because they lack confidence or just that they have not had the opportunity to make choices and be independent. What can practitioners do? Offering two alternatives and asking the child to select one would be a reasonable starting point, then gradually offering one activity and asking, 'is there something else you'd rather do?' would lead children into making their own choices. In addition the best thing would be to explain, 'it's all about having a go and trying things out and having fun.' Many children need the reassurance that if they make mistakes and get things wrong, it doesn't matter – that that is how they learn.

Some children prefer not to go outside to play. They may fear getting hurt or be afraid they won't know how to get into a game. A good idea is to have a safe 'watching seat' where children can stay until they have the confidence to join in. They can then view the bikes and trolleys and decide when they could try them out. Or perhaps they could draw 'big wheels' or other things they see? In my view this is better than offering an alternative activity indoors, but of course it depends on the child and what is causing the fear.

ACTIVITIES IN THE EARLY YEARS SETTING

Many settings organise their rooms into areas or corners that house a range of activities. Some are free choice and some, such as the story corner, allow the children to be gathered together for a group activity. Practitioners change the activities to ensure that the children have a range of experiences and particular ones might be selected as a subtle intervention designed to support children who would benefit from special practice. For example in a baking activity, children have to learn the rules e.g. wash hands, put on aprons, use the spoons to measure ingredients. This helps children with organising and sequencing problems i.e. knowing what comes first then next. And if any children had poor hand strength, the practitioners would be likely to select them to be first to mix the margarine because the firmness would give most resistance and make their fingers work hard.

FIGURE 4.3 Martin baking

Figure 4.3 shows Martin following a recipe. His recipe book is made up of laminated pictures with simple instructions that some children will want to 'read.' He is trusted to use the heaters to melt his chocolate now and his rice crispy cakes will be shared at snack. So he is learning to be in charge and to enjoy sharing. Martin's learning has crossed all aspects of development and his confidence and self-esteem have been strengthened:

- He has also learned to follow a sequence. He plans what comes first and next.
- He understands that written instructions/drawings can guide him without recourse to staff.
- He has 'read' and prepared the ingredients and set them out. This develops his organisational skills.
- He is handling equipment carefully including the heater. This gives him independence although a supervisor will be nearby.
- He is discovering the properties/textures of different ingredients e.g. the stickiness of honey and the changing consistency of items as they melt over heat.
- He is developing altruism if his cake is to be shared.
- He has the satisfaction of completing a task: the patience to wait while the cake cooks (delayed gratification) and the expectation of achieving something that will win praise.

Both Sam and Martin have been engaged in 4-year-old activities that have an 'outcome'. Many children will prefer to be engaged in dressing up or playing with bricks where nothing is actually 'produced.' These are equally valid play activities – just harder to get pictures to show!

Gifted and talented children can show extended learning in the normal play curriculum.

There has been much debate about the difference between giftedness and talent and the competences that are required for children to be nominated into each category. The Edinburgh framework for gifted and talented pupils defined giftedness as 'the untrained and spontaneously expressed natural ability in at least one domain that places the child in the top 15 per cent of his age group'. The key words were 'untrained' and 'naturally expressed' – in any area. Gagne (2001) saw leadership and creative thinking – i.e. unusual ways to solve problems – as his choice of competences.

This is different from being very good at maths and language. In the literature, ability in these competences, along with sports/athletic musical

TABLE 4.3 A synopsis of early years activities showing how the different aspects of development are encouraged

	Home area	Art and craft area	Large construction area	Sand and water trays	Music and dance
Social	• Planning a meal together • Sharing ideas • Waiting to be served	• Discussing ideas for a collage • Sharing resources	• Building together • Sharing ideas and plans	• Planning a road-building scheme – or a water feature with siphons and tubes	• Planning an accompanied dance • Sharing percussion
Intellectual	• 1–1 correspondence in setting tables • Colour matching • Language development	• Learning about mixing colours • Use of different materials and textures	• Organising blocks in height/weight order • Appreciating weights and sizes e.g. 'What will fit?'	• Understanding floating and sinking • Vocabulary extension • Understanding properties of wet and dry sand • Measuring and counting	• Investigating different sounds and how they stimulate different qualities of movement
Emotional	• Role-play – being Dad, Mum, caring for baby	• Appreciating patterns and shapes	• Dealing with frustration when blocks collapse • Pride in completing a construction	• Appreciation of the different elements coming together, e.g. building a fort and a moat	• Appreciating sounds and actions • Enjoying the activities
Moral	• Complying with others' wishes • Making judgements regarding what is right and what is wrong	• Satisfaction in making a gift for someone; or in completing a piece of work	• Looking out for each other when using heavy blocks • Sharing spaces	• Recognising the talents of other children • Considering their wishes and adapting to them	• Identifying preferences • Complying with ideas • Using musical instruments sensitively
Motor	• Handling dishes • Dialling the telephone	• Fine motor control of the brush • Accurate threading • Hand–eye co-ordination	• Lifting and lowering with control • Developing strength and 'finesse' in placing the blocks	• Two hands working together at the midline of the body • Scooping, moulding, firming the sand • Lifting siphons • Control in pouring the water	• Co-ordinating sounds and actions • Balance and control of the body • Developing body and spatial awareness

FIGURE 4.4 After studying some books on design, Anna and Sophie are sharing their ideas and co-operating to produce wallpaper patterns to decorate the house corner

abilities are named as 'talents' rather than gifts because they come about as the result of rigorous teaching and training. Certainly talented pupils perform well above the norm in these domains, but Gagne claimed this was down to enthusiasm, motivation, commitment and rigorous coaching rather than a natural gift. The document also explains that 'quality early years' provision has the potential for challenging and satisfying gifted and talented youngsters'. This is because the children have the freedom to make choices and the time to stay with a creative piece of work because they are not constrained by timetables. They also have the support of practitioners who can answer questions and/or guide them to resources for further study. They may seek resources and compile artifacts, make up a story and tell it to the other children. They can prepare questions to ask on an outing to a theatre or a fire station. This is conceptually different from introducing primary age work, although some parents would like this to happen.

Practitioners have also to explain that mathematical learning is everywhere in the setting. When children fill egg boxes with apples or small toys they are reinforcing the number six. Estimating how many beads will fill a small jar is an introduction to understanding estimating and capacity while arranging them into a pattern to make a necklace needs a basic understanding of symmetry. Siphoning water can be just a messy game for some children but it has the capacity to engage children in real scientific understanding. Appreciating what makes the water flow quickly and dry up to a trickle is one problem and this could lead to finding how the setting/their home is supplied by water. Questions such as 'Where does the water come from?' can provide surprising answers. One child was sure it came out of daddy's hosepipe! Mathematical language develops too. Questions such as 'Who can pour in *more* water?' 'Who can thread the needle *through* the bead?' 'Make the ball stop *inside* the circle' 'Who can make a long thin plasticine snake and who wants to make a short fat one? Let's hold them up to see the difference' develop mathematical understanding. This is contextual learning rather than rote learning that can be based on parroting with no understanding at all!

Often young children can be delighted by being able to count up to ten and find this achievement great fun. But when asked 'Give me two

FIGURE 4.5 Iain is developing his understanding of how snails move; later he will search for a book on 'mini-beasts'

63

pencils', they may look blank. The numbers have not yet encapsulated meaning. This is why numbers appear at the snack table. Children learn they can have two biscuits – and so the number is associated with the food. It is contextually relevant.

When children are intrigued, they can concentrate for a long time. Iain knew to watch rather than touch and to be very gentle if he had to keep the snail safe from falling over the edge. He went on to ask, 'What other creatures move like that? And 'Do other creatures have shells? He wanted to know how a large snail could fit into a small shell and practitioners were glad to find him a children's natural history book!

One child watching Iain was heard exclaiming, 'I want a snail. I like buggery too!' Well he had worked with a wormery and an antery so what was the place where bugs (minibeasts) lived to be called?

PLAY CAN SUPPORT CHILDREN WITH SPECIAL NEEDS TOO

A jingle penned for them can explain some of their apprehensions when they come into the early years setting.

> When I go to school each day,
> I know there's time to play,
> There's lots of toys and girls and boys,
> What shall I do today?
> I'd like to play with the big red truck,
> If there isn't too much noise,
> But usually, with my bad luck,
> It's surrounded by big boys.
> I can't bear messy things like clay,
> And dressing up's no good.
> What does it mean to wear strange clothes?
> I wish I understood!
> The bricks are best; I line them up,
> Red, then white, then blue.
> I love the patterns that they make,
> It's the best thing that I do.
> I really enjoy the water tray,
> I make things sink and float.
> At the sand I build a castle
> Surrounded by a moat.

There are so many things to do
And we get to choose,
And so we win and know that we
Need never, ever, lose!

Christine Macintyre

Play is good for all children and especially perhaps for those who need a little longer to learn, for those who need repeated instructions and for those who do not enjoy freedom or who lack planning and organisational

TABLE 4.4 Some difficulties that cross 'labels' and make playing hard work

Intellectual difficulties

- Not knowing what to do
- Not being able to follow the unwritten rules of someone's game, so not contributing appropriate ideas to take the play forward
- Having a poor memory, so forgetting yesterday's play ideas
- Having too many ideas but not being able to plan or organise play resources or ideas
- Not understanding/being able to cope with changes in routine

Social difficulties

- Being unable to communicate effectively
- Poor articulation, making interaction difficult
- Being too timid to join in
- Being reluctant to share or wait for a turn
- Snatching rather than asking
- Preferring to be alone – all the time
- Only wanting what someone else has

Movement difficulties

- Not being able to balance on stepping stones or on a bike
- Being clumsy and knocking into others
- Being too active and out of control
- Being uncoordinated, especially at the midline of the body, so spilling water, messing up puzzles
- Inability to grasp/release items
- Unable to throw or catch a ball
- Body build difficulties, making children avoid movement practices

Emotional difficulties

- Being unable to understand pretending
- Lack of imagination to develop play ideas
- Poor concentration; little focus or staying power
- Inability to understand what someone else is thinking or feeling, so responding inappropriately
- Not responding at all
- Completely immersed in own solitary play
- Aggressive when thwarted
- Poor empathy and altruism, so unable to understand other children's perspectives

65

skills. Although children with difficulties find many or even all of these competences demanding, they have to acquire them. Play allows practice, often repeated practice free from the stress of having to finish something and having to get it right! There is no time pressure.

At this early age children with Down's syndrome are socially able and they will interact happily with their peers who often take a delight in caring for them. Indeed they can do too much for them and this is usually accepted with a smile!! As well as encouraging independence, practitioners have to make sure children with Down's syndrome can hear because their smaller ear passages can get blocked by mucous. If this is not treated, (usually by having grommets fitted), the children's speech can be affected for if they have not heard clearly, how can they reproduce the sound? For these children communication is often easier by gesture, but speaking must be gently encouraged too. As they mature they gain strength in the muscles in their tongues and soft palates and this can help clarity/diction.

N.B. Children who have Down's syndrome should not be allowed to do forward rolls even on a thick mat until the possibility of their having cervical instability has been checked. They should not have pressure on their necks. Otherwise they can join in all the activities happily and often they do so with gusto and charm.

Children on the autistic spectrum need a tight routine because of their difficulty in anticipating events and not being able to read the non-verbal skills of others. They will play most happily alone, for they won't be able to explain the rules of their game nor understand what is involved in playing with another child. They may select a favourite toy and to the unwary seem to be playing, e.g. they may choose a red truck and spin the wheels, but closer observation will reveal that this action doesn't turn into a 'real' game – there is no role play or symbolism (e.g. pretending one thing is another – using a yo-yo as a dog) or development of a story e.g. their truck helping to carry sand to build a dam. They are unlikely to use the pronoun 'I' and this hinders clear communication. Of course these observations will depend on the level of severity of the condition.

Children with Attention Deficit Hyperactivity Disorder (ADHD) can concentrate for spells if they are really interested in what they are doing. So the choice element of play is very suitable. The freedom to go outside and 'let off steam' is also useful and can calm children who are driven by impulsive behaviour. There is also such a variety of activity that short-term interests can be catered for. The children have more difficulty being quiet and calm at story time so it is helpful if practitioners try to choose stories that are short and if possible based on their interests.

Some children later diagnosed with dyslexia may have poor balance and may have difficulty beating out a rhythm on a drum. Again their hearing should be checked because many children have poor discriminatory hearing, i.e. they are not deaf but have difficulty differentiating between different sounds. Asking the children to listen to simple rhyming words and picking out the odd one out e.g. cat, bat, fish, rat can pinpoint difficulties.

Children who have the early symptoms of dyspraxia will be likely to be clumsy and disorganised. They will be late for everything and find difficulty organising their resources. They may have memory problems e.g. forgetting who is coming to collect them as well as what they did yesterday. For them the lack of time pressure is salutary as well as having practitioners to help them check that they have all their belongings ready to go home. For more information on special needs conditions read Macintyre (2014) – the companion book to this one.

The chapter finishes by showing the learning potential in seven areas. These charts can be photocopied and used as tools for observation and assessment.

Intellectual

Mother, father, baby, visitor, pet dog — Role play

Fruit, seeds, nuts, sandwich fillings, pitta/brown bread — Choosing healthy foods for tea

Menus for lunch — where to buy vegetables/flour etc. — Discussing what to buy

Spoonfuls at baking time — One-to-one correspondence

Setting the table, matching, sorting — Counting

What different visitors, e.g. aliens, would like to eat — Imagining

Movement (motor)

Dressing and undressing — Doll/baby hanging up aprons, coats

Preparing food — Baking, chopping, washing, mixing, shredding, spreading, arranging on plates

'Ironing' — Flattening and folding tea cloths

'Writing' — Picture 'invitations' to the tea party

Learning in the house corner

Social

Drinks, food and treats — Sharing

Choosing favourite foods for baby/visitor/alien — Caring

Passing plates, pouring juice — Taking turns

Waiting, saying 'thank you' — Being helper; being a guest

Talking with all the people at tea — Communicating

Emotional

Appreciating — Taking responsibility / Being 'in charge'

Gaining satisfaction — when 'guests' have a lovely time

Empathising — with guests who might be timid

Overcoming fears and worries — Trying new tasks — phobias reduced

Being able to stay near another person — Tolerating sitting beside a child

Intellectual

Understanding that clothes can change characters — Role-playing

What shall I be? — Decision-making

Will the costume fit? — Problem-solving

Taking part in dramatic play, e.g. being a fireman — Acting

What resources will match my costume? — Planning

Movement (motor)

Dressing and changing clothes — Fastening buttons, zips

Using resources — Floor mop (Cinderella), tutu (ballet dancer)

Making resources — Crowns, necklaces, wands and other props

Learning in the dressing-up corner

Listening to their wishes — understanding perspective — Assisting others to dress up

a) In waiting for a costume
b) In building a drama sequence — Turn-taking

That characters change, and altering motivations to suit — Understanding

Someone else's ideas/ plan and giving praise — Following and adapting ploys

Having confidence — a) to join in b) to become someone else and take on their role

Empathising

Understanding different roles

Avoiding suppressing fears — by acting them out in a safe place

Gaining satisfaction — from taking on another preferred role

Social

Emotional

Intellectual

The sequence of actions — Planning

Equipment and resources — Organising

Remembering what comes first then next — Sequencing

Completing the action — Doing

Estimating distances/heights — Judging

Knowing when to jump, throw, chase etc. — Timing

Movement (motor)

Balancing — and after jumping

Coordinating actions, control — Slowing down and stopping at the correct time

Transitions — Joining two actions together

Gross motor skills — Crawling, climbing, walking, running, jumping, rolling*

*pencil rolls only for children with Down's syndrome

Outdoor play on large apparatus

Learning to let others go first (developing understanding of how others feel) — Waiting Taking turns

Watching others; copying good ideas on seesaw — Cooperating

Ball skills, e.g. throwing/catching/aiming — Being part of a team

Matching movements; fitting in spaces — Making up a movement game in twos

Paying attention — Remembering and carrying out instructions

Gaining confidence — Becoming motivated to try more movement sequences

Endorphins working

Releasing tension/energy/stress — Running, jumping, wheeling

Reducing cortisol — Calming down

Social

Emotional

Intellectual

Rhythm **Learning**

Different qualities **Accompanying**
of sound

Different instruments **Recognising**

the beats **Counting**

the different instruments **Naming**

words of songs **Planning**

the number of instruments **Organising**

Movement (motor)

Playing Different instruments

Controlling sounds

Coordinating Two hands doing different
things

Two hands doing the same
things (cymbals)

Controlling length of sound

Accompanying a dancer

Learning in the music corner

Appreciating Tone

Understanding a) that black notes are symbols for
sounds

b) how sounds can represent ideas,
e.g. fire crackling, rain pattering

Playing together **Cooperating**

basic compositions **Sharing**

to others making sounds **Listening**

for instruments **Caring**

within the group about **Talking**
the sounds

Investigating Different sounds and how they
can make sound story

Responding to sounds

Gaining confidence in playing and listening

Social

Emotional

Intellectual

Beach/golf course   Where is sand used?

Egg timer (fine sand)   Timing

Measuring/estimating

Spades of sand   Counting

Choosing correct tools   Selecting
for the job

Empty; full   Language
Heavy; light; overflowing
More than; less than

Properties of
sand

Wet/dry/runny sand discussions, e.g.
a) is it easier to run on   Discussions
wet or dry sand?
b) what kind of sand is
best for building?

Movement (motor)

Gross motor   Using spoon/spade
manipulative skills   to fill bucket or tipper
truck

Fine motor   Decorating the sandcastle

Patting   Building castles in a pail

Smoothing   Making sides firm

Finger
strengthening   ruts

Coordination at the midline of the
body; control in building/pouring
water

Learning at the sand tray

Making a moat   Cooperating
in building
roads together

Carrying water and pouring
carefully to fill moat

Building roads and   Gathering resources/
making a village   discussing plans

Letting more children
join the game

Sharing plans and
developing ideas together

Appreciation   of effort needed to build

Tolerating   feel of sand; getting grubby

Visualising   the bigger plan, e.g. imagining
living in a castle

Empathising   with the hard work
builders do

Social

Emotional

Intellectual

Building a cave that   Learning about
won't collapse; or a   floating and sinking
paper boat that will float
in the moat   Problem-solving

Dry and wet sand —   Estimating levels;
selecting and adapting   pailfuls needed

of water/ice/freezing   Understanding
melting disappearing   changing properties

Displacement of water when blocks
are added to the tray; submerging

Floating and sinking   Investigating

Movement (motor)

Placing   small world figures

Controlling   water flow in
filling/emptying tubes,
syphons

Building   wet sand; strengthening
hands, arms and shoulders

Developing coordination at the
midline of the body

Learning at the water tray and sand tray

Social

A day at the seaside   Discussing
Anticipating
A sandcastle with a moat   Cooperating to
build a scene

Splashing water   Looking out for
Scattering sand   others

Ideas and equipment   Sharing

Emotional

Enjoying   the feel of water at different
temperatures

Splashing, swirling, mixing colours

Making firm sandcastles

Creating   'miniatures' of real events,
e.g diggers

Appreciating   ideas and developments

Intellectual

Vegetables/fruit/flowers   Recognising plants in the garden

Sizes of plants   Comparing

Speed of growth

Providing food — making fat balls, bird bath/table   Attracting birds and mini-beasts to the garden

Learning about poisonous plants — deciduous plants

Safety in garden equipment   Safety issues

Keeping the garden tidy/ free from litter   Responsibility

Learning what fruits/veg. will grow — and what dishes they will make, e.g that chips are cut-up potatoes!   Fruits / Vegetables

Movement (motor)

Planting   bulbs and following their growing cycle

Watering   Carrying a watering can

Pouring   the water gently so as not to disturb plants

Stepping   gently to avoid damaging the plants

Controlling   Scattering seeds carefully

Covering   delicate plants with fleece in the winter

Learning in the garden area

Collecting conkers to see the prickles (to keep the seed secure)   Collecting seeds together in the autumn

Preparing a patch of soil   Working together

Plants and seeds for tubs   Choosing/discussing

Taking care of a plot together   Having responsibility in twos or threes

Social

Appreciating   how beautiful plants are; how delicate plants are

Watching   the process of seeds maturing and growing

Tending   Watering, feeding, supporting plants

Observing   Slow growth — delayed gratification

Emotional

Chapter 5

Understanding motor development

Movement is the first aspect to be discussed as 'Movement is the child's first language' (Piaget 1954) and so many competences e.g. speaking clearly, writing depend on movement skills. From the start the children's self esteem is boosted if they can communicate through stretching out to be lifted, by the praise they receive when they can crawl and walk and run and achieve their motor milestones. Poor movement competence can also be the very first sign that development is not on track and so early interventions that are proven to have the best chance of success can be brought into play.

The chapter has been organised around questions that practitioners often ask.

Q. Why is being able to move well in different environments so important?

Many young children love to run and jump, swing and climb and they do this with pleasure and with ease. They skip along pavements and hop over the lines that cross their paths. Many continue their active pursuits and enjoy sports training to a high level. In so doing, they are keeping fit and finding a life full of zest. Over more recent years, however, as computer games and safety concerns have intruded, a widespread concern that many of our young children are unfit and overweight has developed. This general change in lifestyle can lead children to avoid the very activities that help to keep them healthy. Both parents being out at work may also result in ready-prepared meals (which usually have a higher salt and fat content) being served more regularly than before. So an increasing number of children are obese; and this in turn has negative effects on their health, their self-esteem and their willingness to be active. Some of the headlines about this trend can be alarming. For example, 'The 10-fold increase in children with diabetes is the tip of the iceberg' (*Telegraph* 28 February 2006, based on a Department of Health report). The article goes on to explain: 'weight-related metabolic syndromes such as high blood pressure, increased cholesterol and fat in the blood are affecting 60,000 children.'

Q. Why should this be?

Due to safety concerns, many children are kept indoors rather than 'getting out to play'. This means they are not building a repertoire of movement skills, and this early lack of practice hampers all of their life skills too.

This is because balance, co-ordination and control of the body are essential if tasks of everyday living are to be efficient. Speaking clearly, zipping a coat, spreading at snack time, using the pincer grip to write and draw, cutting out and colouring in – these are just some of a huge number of movement skills and so it is not difficult to see how poor movement skills affect all aspects of development.

Thankfully, children are now being urged to walk to school, to play out of doors, to play the old-fashioned games such as hopscotch (or 'peevers' as it is known in Scotland). Supermarkets that gave out 'computers for schools' programmes are now distributing tokens for activity clubs. And in many areas where there are few facilities for sport, or little time or money to provide activity clubs, or where children present with difficulties that concern the staff, schools are setting up compensatory movement programmes.

Q. Will this counteract the damage that has been done?

The new moves are gratifying, but what is essential is to provide opportunities for all our children to enjoy movement to the extent that they want to keep moving, for this stimulates bone density, cardiovascular health and endomorphins. Endomorphins provide that important, feel-good factor that keeps children confident and smiling.

Movement is part of everything we do, from opening our eyes in the morning, to speaking clearly and modulating the tone and pitch of our speech, to carrying out all the activities of daily living and learning. If anyone doubts this, then trying to list activities that do not involve movement can be a salutary experience.

Being able to run and kick a ball, or climb, or ride a bike are the activities children want to do, as well as and, very importantly, at the

FIGURES 5.1–5.2 Activities where balance, co-ordination and control are essential for success

same time as their friends. If they can't, their friends notice and unfortunately this can lead to teasing. Children who 'can't do' get left out of activities where competence is important and they are not chosen for games. Being part of a group also helps children to be independent. Being judged inadequate because of poor movement does their self-esteem significant damage and may prevent the children trying to improve.

Q. Somehow parents don't seem to recognise how important movement is?

That's very true, but when they realise that a good sense of balance helps writing and that the fine motor skills required in music also help mathematics (because a part of each fingertip used in playing an instrument is connected to the maths area in the cerebral cortex), then movement takes its rightful place as the key to learning.

Q. How many children find it difficult to move well?

A surprising 6–10 per cent of all children find movement so difficult that all aspects of living and learning are compromised (Dyspraxia Foundation 2001). Boys appear on this list much more than girls, in a ratio of 4:1 or 5:1.

Q. So, what can practitioners do to support children who have problems?

It is vital to find out the real cause. It may be inability to do the movement itself, and this could be due to a neurological cause (e.g. poor myelination), which impacts on balance, co-ordination and control, or it may be the planning and organising (the mental preparation that precedes an action) that hinders the outcome.

So practitioners must:

- observe carefully, so that they can record what is amiss;
- understand why the children are experiencing these difficulties, based on evidence gleaned from observations;
- design movement programmes which will help the children's development and help them to practise regularly every single day.

MOVEMENT ACTIVITIES, WITH OBSERVATION/ TEACHING POINTS

Q. What skills need to be developed?

Activities to develop body and spatial awareness, balance, co-ordination and control should be part of everyday practice for they are essential prerequisites in every fine motor, gross motor and manipulative skill. A small sample can be seen in Table 5.1.

TABLE 5.1 Some fine, gross and manipulative motor skills

Fine motor (using the small muscle groups)	Gross motor (using the large muscle groups)	Everyday manipulative skills (using both muscle groups)
Fastening buttons/tying laces	Crawling, walking, running and jumping, hopping, turning corners, i.e. all the basic movement patterns	Cleaning teeth; wiping at the toilet. Writing, painting, drawing, threading, spreading at snack, picking things up and letting go
Articulating words. Using gestures to communicate meaning	Crawling though a tunnel	Opening the door. Packing a bag/lunch box. Organising equipment
Picking up objects using the pincer (tripod) grip	Throwing and catching/kicking a ball	Tidying up. Manipulating a mouse/keyboard. Texting etc.
Letting objects go	Climbing stairs	Eating at mealtimes. Using a knife and fork
Stirring, pouring, mixing	Hopping	Fastening up a jacket
Writing and drawing	Skipping	Jumping onto a bus
Doing a jigsaw; using Lego	Building bricks	Riding a bike

Q. **This is a much wider view of movement than we had thought initially. We were thinking about activities like climbing on the frame or rolling on the mats. Maybe it would be a good idea to make a list of movements that are especially important in our own setting? We could use that as a focus for observation. But how would we record improvement?**

You could use the symbols 0 (meaning can't do), 1 (OK) and 2 (very proficient) to record competence, and then recheck progress every two weeks or so to see whether improvement has been made. This is why it is very important to include the date when recording observations. The important thing is to keep the records very simple for children who can cope, but to record exact details for those who find movement difficult. It's also important to try to extend the able children, perhaps by asking them to explain what they plan to do. For this they need some movement language, e.g. 'I'm going "under" the rope and "through" the hoop to stand "opposite" the tree'. So movement helps maths too! Also remember you can't see every child every day. Make a careful list so that you include them all over a weekly or fortnightly slot.

But, of course, being able to do all these things doesn't happen overnight and there is a developmental sequence that differentiates 'performance' over the age range, e.g. while 3-year-olds might still use the step-together pattern in climbing stairs, 4-year-olds should be able to use the one-foot-at-a-time action, provided they have stairs at home.

Q. When should practitioners begin to assess children's movement skills?

1. In a general way: this should be as soon as possible, to note things the children find straightforward and actions they find difficult.
2. More specifically: once the children are at ease in their surroundings; when they are familiar with any apparatus, and have built relationships with their practitioners. Then close observation can reveal perceptual or sensory difficulties as well as the more obvious movement ones.

Of course, children have different experiences before coming to the early years setting/school as well as different temperaments, and these will influence the way they approach new activities. This means that assessments should not happen once but be repeated over a period of time. They can then contribute towards a profile of achievement for passing on to 'big school' or be used as evidence to speed access to expert help. If additional learning needs are suspected, it is helpful to video the children (parental permission will be needed), because visuals are often clearer than written descriptions. Video also allows recordings to be reviewed and shared so that more/less experienced eyes can give practitioners confidence in making decisions about intervention.

Q. Are there other things that should be checked out first?

Before starting to assess, it can be revealing to consider whether other factors, even inflexible shoes, may prevent the children moving well.

TABLE 5.2 An observational record of basic movement patterns

Crawling 16 April 2013	Standing/sitting still 18 April 2013	Running and jumping 22 April 2013
Rowan (2 yrs 6 mths) 0 – still unable to balance on all fours; suspect lack of arm strength – test hand grip, shoulder stability	1 – improving but needs time to focus	
Charlene (3 yrs 4 mths) 2	2	1 – still rushes take-off – lacks sense of where her feet are – do foot awareness jingles
Martin (4 yrs 6 mths) 2	2 – but can't wait	2 – now ask him what he needs to do to jump higher
Jilly (5 yrs 6 mths) 1 – prefers to pull along on her front	2 – but appears solidly fixed to the spot. She collapses into herself – aim to develop tummy and back strength (spinning cone)	0 – can't cope with the co-ordination demands – practise jumping on her own

If this is not done, then interventions to support the children may be based on incorrect information. The list shown in Figure 5.3 offers some guidance.

Q. OK, but what are the questions that we should ask about movement itself?

A first checklist is suggested in Figure 5.4.

When staff suspect a problem, then arranging the big apparatus to highlight the difficulty can provide evidence of whether it is or is not there. When one boy was thought to have poor arm strength, the staff put out a long tunnel so that he had to crawl through, then pull out at the end. What happened was that the child used his head as a lever to pull himself through. He had developed a strategy to compensate, but hiding the problem was not going to make it go away.

Does the child have	Yes	No	Comment/ severity/ medication other aids required
Sensory difficulties, e.g.			
1 Poor balance?			
2 Poor hearing?			
3 Restricted vision?			
4 Allergies?			
5 Asthma?			
Communication difficulties, e.g.			
1 Understanding?			
2 Articulating?			
3 Explaining?			
Personality/behaviour difficulties, e.g.			
1 Shyness?			
2 Aggression?			
3 Withdrawn?			
4 Slow to warm up?			
5 Low self-esteem?			

FIGURE 5.3 Differentiating between fine, gross and manipulative skills

Can the child	Yes	No	Comment: e.g. is clumsy, falls over easily
Move with control? i.e. judge the correct amount of strength and speed that is required?			
Crawl, using the cross-lateral pattern?			
Cope with steps-up and -down?			
Judge drops safely? Leave the ground (jump, hop or skip)?			
Consistently use the same hand/ foot?			
Work confidently at/ cross the midline of the body?			
Change direction easily?			
Look in control of their own body?			

FIGURE 5.4 A checklist of important indicators of motor development

These preliminary baseline assessments are very useful. Often parents may (mistakenly) not be too concerned about poor movement competence until the child finds writing impossible. The difficulties will have been there in the child – they don't suddenly appear – but in the early years, parents tend to fasten coats, tie laces and carry bags just to save time and so the children's difficulties aren't immediately apparent.

Q. So how does movement hamper writing?

Writing is a movement skill. The child should sit in a balanced position with feet steady on the floor and with a desk at elbow height. An inclined writing board can prevent unnecessary and confusing movements of the head, and a thick pencil with a special grip (there are many on the market to suit all hands) can support the tripod or pincer grip. It is also important that the sitting position of right- and left-handed children is considered to save elbows clashing and possibly tempers fraying. Right-handed children should be on the right.

Sometimes, if writing letters back to front persists, it can indicate a lack of hand dominance, i.e. not knowing which hand to use, which should be in place by age 3 years. Practitioners can help children to decide and then remind them to use their more proficient side when they try other activities.

In a game of tossing a beanbag into a waste-paper bin, Grethe was asked: 'Which hand scored the most goals?' Once she was sure, she was gently reminded of her choice at painting, threading and spreading.

And so there are simple strategies to solve specific difficulties, but when these persist, a daily movement programme is the best way forward.

Q. When can I do a programme? Does it need to be in one block each day?

Not necessarily. When you want to use large apparatus then it is best to have a planned time, so that someone has responsibility for checking all the safety points in advance of the children arriving.

Q. How do you bring out the intellectual component with very young children?

You might ask the most able children to help with the organisation and resourcing, setting tasks such as:

- Please help to set the table for snack. Three people sit at each table . . .
- We have four children playing outside. Can you set out the bikes and balls?
- Can you bring the book we read yesterday over to the story corner?
- Can you sort the coloured bands into bundles of the same colour for me?
- Can you sort this bundle out so that I have the same number of red, blue and green bands?
- What apparatus should we choose for balancing today?
- Can you make up the rules for a game that uses a big ball, but has benches for goals instead of a net? Think of how the game starts, how a goal is scored and what you need to do to ensure the game stays safe for all the players.

Movement activities can be interspersed with sedentary work, even within the confines of a classroom. If there is restricted space, allowing one table of children to march in and out the spaces without touching can give respite and help concentration.

Q. Can you help us with more ideas for activities?

The following ideas cover gross movements, fine motor skills and manipulative skills. I'm sure that, once you start, ideas will come flooding in (see ideas in Macintyre and McVitty (2004)). It's important to remember that even very simple movements (e.g. walking along a bench) should be done well, before complications (e.g. carrying a hoop, or stepping over beanbags) are introduced.

ACTIVITIES TO HELP PROMOTE BODY AND SPATIAL AWARENESS, BALANCE, CO-ORDINATION AND CONTROL

Note: The aim of any programme is to have children improve their basic movement patterns and to be able to adapt these in different environments, e.g. a child can progress from learning to crawl on the floor to crawling along a bench, then an inclined bench, and then crawling up stairs, for the crawling and the climbing pattern are one and the same. The changed environment adds variety and challenge. If children 'cannot do', then simplifying the resources (e.g. catching a balloon that travels more slowly than a ball), or modifying the environment (e.g. having the child kick a ball into an empty goal rather than having to outwit a goalie) can give a positive start.

KEY FACTORS IN DEVELOPING EFFICIENT MOVEMENT

Body awareness – children have to be able to feel where their body parts are

Simon says and similar games

(See Table 5.3 for an example of 'Simon says'.) These games are always well liked and they are excellent for helping children with poor body

TABLE 5.3 'Simon says'

Simon says (copying and then without copying)	Look out for	Help
Put two hands on your head.	Slow reaction: two arms moving at different speeds.	Use body parts the children can see, e.g. knees, toes.
Stretch two arms into the sky. Look up to see your fingers (stars twinkling suggest movement).	Children overbalancing, especially when head position changes and fingers move. Bent arms – one or both.	1. Stand against wall to help balance. 2. Face wall and climb fingers up (Incy wincy spider).
Sit down and stretch your legs out in front. Lean back on your hands. Move feet towards and away together then alternately.	Slumping trunks, heads poking forward. Head nodding as feet move. Inability to do the alternative foot action.	Count out 'Hello toes, Goodbye toes' to help children recognise the rhythm of the action. Remind them to 'sit tall with long straight backs'.
Crossing the midline. Put one hand on the other knee. Use twirling ribbons to make figures of eight across the body.	Children who can't cross the midline.	Give the children a beanbag in each hand. Try 'semaphore' type actions where one hand stands still but the other moves to meet it.

awareness recognise and feel where their different body parts are. These activities develop the children's sense of body boundary too. This means that they recognise where their bodies end and the outside world begins, an important skill which contributes to deft movement and safety, e.g. placing a cup firmly on a table (rather than precariously on the edge), or recognising where to stop at the kerb.

Many early years jingles are based on promoting body awareness, e.g. 'Heads, shoulders, knees and toes', 'Under the spreading chestnut tree', 'Tap time' (in Macintyre, 2003).

Stressing movement during everyday activities in the early years setting

As the children are engaged in their early years activities, comments such as 'Hold your arm into your side and you'll be strong enough to pour the water into the jug without spilling' or 'Look how close together your hands are when you are threading/spreading' can help develop body awareness.

Q. How do we make children aware of their backs?

Ideally, use a spinning cone. To make the cone turn, the children must begin the action by leaning back and pushing, then the abdominal muscles must work hard till the back takes over again.

Table 5.4 shows some other ideas.

Q. If children appear floppy, how can we make them stronger? Or if they are stiff, what then?

Table 5.5 shows some ideas. Some resistance is needed to make the muscles work harder while helping the child's mobility needs limbs to move through a greater range, e.g. use twirling ribbons to encourage the children to stretch through the full range of movement. Pulling through water in the swimming pool or even in the water tray, creating roads in wet sand and moulding wet clay are all useful ideas. If the children are unhappy with the texture of clay, they can often tolerate 'Theraputty'. Theraputty is a clean malleable substance (which children who dislike 'dirty clay' are usually happy to use). There are five strengths, so the density of the material can be changed as strength develops. The children can pull it, mould it and stretch it. One enjoyable task is to find hidden treasure inside a ball

TABLE 5.4 Some other ideas for movement activities

Activity: Angels in the snow	Look out for	Help
Lie on the floor – open and close legs feeling the backs of the legs on the floor	Children who cannot move their legs together without looking to see what is happening	Do the action sitting first so that they can see the movement and internalise the feel of it
Sweep the arms overhead (backs of arms on the floor)	Bent arms – suggest they turn palms up – this pulls the shoulders back	If the arm sweep is difficult, allow the children to hold a beanbag in each hand
Do both actions together	Can they join two hands together above their heads and bump two feet together when they meet at the midline of the body?	Give plenty of time. Check shoulder rigidity. DO NOT FORCE any action – ask for physiotherapy if child cannot relax the shoulders
Children lie in a line or in a circle. As they sweep hands up they should touch their neighbour's hand. Feet can touch as the legs sweep apart	Check timing and awareness of movement to the side. Can the children time the action without looking?	Check backs don't lift from the floor – if so the stretch is too wide – narrow the activity

of Theraputty. This involves the children in lots of pulling, which strengthens fingers, forearms and even shoulders.

Gross motor skills

Crawling (to help co-ordination, balance and spatial orientation)

See Table 5.6 for some crawling activities. Teach the crawling action using a jingle, e.g.

> Right hand, left knee on we go
> Left hand right knee, who can show?
> Crawling forwards 1, 2, 3
> You can do it easily!

TABLE 5.5 Some other ideas for strengthening activities

Activity	Look out for	Help
Popping bubble paper	Fingers without sufficient strength	Pull fingers through water; build castles in the sand – give lots of strengthening work
Winding a yo-yo	Children who cannot work with two hands doing different things at the midline of the body	Use large jigsaws or puzzles where the action happens at or crosses the midline. Woodwork is popular
Threading beads	Children who close one eye – check whether this happens at other times – check with optician	Begin in a sitting position to minimise balance demands. This is an aiming practice – check pincer/tripod grip
Nursery darts	Check stance for the start of an overarm throw (opposite foot forward)	Transfer of weight from back to front foot. Call out rhythm 1, . . . 3; 3 is throw
Quickly transferring balls, shuttlecocks, reels, etc. (small objects of different sizes and shapes) from one pail to another (time challenge)	Difficulty in grasping and letting go	Increase the space between the pails. This means the required hand actions are slower and less demanding
Batting a shuttlecock with a small wooden bat	Children who can't time the contact – begin with very small hits	Support the hand to keep the face of the bat flat. The sound should help the rhythm
Playing an old piano	Children who can't press the keys or who use too much strength	Check whether some fingers in particular lack strength. If so have activities such as rolling/modelling clay available

FIGURE 5.5 Making handprints helps develop hand awareness and finger strength

When 'Kicking horses' (an activity like a handstand with one knee remaining on the ground and the other leg swung upwards) is used,

Make your arms and hands so strong,
Stretch one leg out, make it long
Swing it up now, really high,
Look – it nearly hits the sky!

Note: Using jingles helps to develop the children's sense of rhythm, which is important in all movement, as well as in speaking, writing and reading. It also helps mathematical skills, e.g. learning times tables.

TABLE 5.6 Some crawling activities

Activity	Look out for	Help
First of all, ask the children to take up the crawling (table) position. This is a safe position where balance is not difficult. The children feel secure.	Children who can't keep a flat back. Wobbly limbs – arms or legs – children who sit back or topple to the side.	Place a beanbag on the small of the back – ask the children to keep it steady there. Emphasise strong arms and legs.
Move the body from side to side or forwards/backwards if they can keep the beanbag in position – then they can try to toss the beanbag off by straightening their legs. They should always come back to the crawling (table) position.	Children who can't regain the table position after moving – they may have to sit back or their arms may collapse.	Strengthening work for arms and legs. Check if children can't move weight forward onto arms (which should stay straight and strong).
In the table position again, the children can pick up beanbags from the floor and toss them into a bin.	Children who can't sweep arms rhythmically or who have to arch their backs to allow arms to go overhead	Physiotherapy help should be sought to ease stiff shoulders

LISTS OF ACTIVITIES TO DEVELOP FINE MOTOR SKILLS

Finger awareness: finger, hand, arm and shoulder strengthening

1. It is essential that children develop dexterity, i.e. being able to handle small objects with control. This comes through practice in manipulating objects that provide some resistance (strengthening work) and learning to use the pincer grip.

    To do this, children need to become aware of how they are using their fingers, hands and arms. They also have to be helped to develop hand dominance.

▉ TABLE 5.7 More activities (1)

Activity	Note	Help
Rolling sideways from the crawling position	This is a safety practice that should first happen on mats. From the crawling or table position the children should tuck one arm through the other, follow it with their head and roll over onto their shoulder and back, sustaining enough momentum to roll right round to kneeling. The children should understand that they are taking their weight on the rounded padded bits and that elbows, the points of shoulders and knees need to be protected.	Safety in landing The children need to realise that this skill, i.e. learning to meet the ground safely, will protect them should they fall. They must not fall on outstretched arms else jarring or even clavicle breakage may occur.
Pencil rolls	Can the children stretch out while keeping their arms rounded into their bodies?	Ask, 'Can you push your toes long?', 'Do you feel where they are?'

2. It is vital that children learn to use two hands at the midline of the body – preferably doing different things, e.g. opening a jar, unscrewing nuts on a bolt, or threading beads. This is bilateral integration. They also have to be able to cross the midline. Figure-of-eight actions, e.g. drawing in the air – perhaps of the first letter of their name – helps this.

3. Reflecting on existing activities in the light of promoting strength and dexterity often shows that some minor organisational change means that they can provide a greater pay-off, e.g. at baking time, let those with poor hand strength be the first to mix the butter and sugar for there is more resistance when the butter is hard.

4. Rolling out dough, using scone cutters (gingerbread men) and placing the dough on baking trays – then eating the results – gives a satisfying sequence of events. Stressing the order helps planning and organising.

TABLE 5.8 More activities (2)

Activity	Check	Help
Walking	Poise, balance and control. The shoulders should be relaxed and low with the arms swinging naturally.	Count out a rhythm if the stride pattern is unequal.
Stepping over bands on the floor	Check the smooth transfer of weight.	
Walking in straight lines, forwards and backwards, then along curves and then with abrupt changes of direction	Note the children who can't change direction. If their toes are pointing in, the whole position of the leg will hinder the change.	Make children aware of placing their foot – look at footprints in the sand. Emphasise toes forward. If this 'hen-toed' action persists, seek physiotherapy help.
Walking through the space made by two facing benches. The activity begins with the benches far apart and gradually being moved together.	The aim is for the children to be aware of objects at their side and to judge the width of their body/ movement pattern in relation to the available space. (This develops spatial awareness and laterality or sidedness.)	Children who are tentative because they cannot see if they will be able to get through the space. Add other 'getting through activities', e.g. passing a hoop over their head to the floor. This lets them judge the space around them.

5. Mashing potatoes with a potato masher can strengthen the shoulders, arms and hands. The children can then mould the mashed potatoes into balls (adding cheese that they have grated) to make croquettes, roll the croquettes in egg and breadcrumbs and pop them in the oven to make a tasty snack.

Dramatic ideas to show a change of quality in walking

Build small group (dramatic) activities based on walking. In these the quality of the walk should change. For example:

1. On a cold frosty morning walk briskly to school.
   - Blow out to make 'frosty breath'. Blow on cupped hands. Shake tingling fingers (these actions can challenge balance).

- Swoop arms round to keep warm (hand and back awareness).
- See a friend and wave. Run over to join hands and jump up and down together to keep warm.

2. It is very hot in the forest. You are trying to spot butterflies and humming birds. You mustn't make a sound.
   - Prowl quietly through the undergrowth (slow careful walking at a low level).
   - Use big sweeping actions to clear a path (balance challenge).
   - Curl up quietly and listen to the humming sounds (awareness of rounded backs).
   - Notice a snake slithering through the undergrowth.
   - Jump up and rush away – leap up into your tree house.

This can be built up into a dramatic dance if different children take different parts, e.g. humming birds, butterflies, snakes, leopards, etc. The children can describe a series of events, and the teacher can add descriptive words linking a class theme and supporting literacy development.

Many more ideas are in *Jingle Time* (see Macintyre, 2003).

As children learn to move, they learn about how to control their bodies and keep them safe. They learn how to run and skip with others and how to catch and kick a ball. These skills allow them to take part in activities with others so their social development benefits. And, as they grow and make judgements about how to care for themselves, there are intellectual and moral elements (e.g. if I keep fit and learn about nutrition, I won't need hospital resources) in this too. So, while each aspect of development is worthy of separate study, analysis is best seen in the context of synthesis, for children use them all together all of the time.

Chapter 6

Understanding social development

A group of early years practitioners was asked to name 'the most important things they wished their children could do' and after a lengthy discussion they compiled the list shown in Table 6.1. They agreed that social development was critically important and their questions and answers are shared below.

Q. Why should social development take priority?

Well, social skills are the stepping stones if you like – if you can trust children not to hit each other and share the resources without squabbling and breaking them, then you have time to concentrate on

TABLE 6.1 Some social skills

Respecting each other and the toys and other resources they have to play with (Simon)	Being kind to one another (Sally) Learning to take turns (Amy) Caring and sharing (Megan)
Learning to watch out for one another – to be aware of safety issues, especially when playing outside (Carol)	Learning to be independent by deciding what they want to do, gathering all the things they need and getting on with it (Jo)
Learning to cope when they get bumped or when pieces of work disappoint them (Dave)	Listening to each other and following another's lead (Amy)
Coping with the routine of the day – knowing what comes next (Omar)	Having a friend and being able to share that friend with others (Fran)

(The practitioners' names, in brackets, are given to ease referring back to the list).

teaching them something, but if you have to stop fights and bickering all the time, then nothing gets done. **(Simon)**

Q. How do you establish this kind of working atmosphere?

We try to act as role models, keeping calm and praising those who are behaving well. We hope the others will copy them. If they don't, then explaining why you are upset or disappointed is always better than being cross. **(Sally)**

'And as the children's temperaments are enhanced or diminished by these early interactions and how their inborn capacities develop depends ultimately on the type of experiences they will encounter' (Robinson 2011), then the importance of these being supportive and encouraging cannot be over emphasised.

Q. What should you do if children already have good social skills? Should you develop these further or concentrate on other aspects of their development?

Even if some children appear to have developed sophisticated social skills, there are always ways to take their understanding forward. Jo was anxious to share her thoughts. She explained,

We have a boy, Odie, who comes from what we would say was a disadvantaged background if we only thought about material things, but socially, he is tops! Despite some language difficulties, he has learned how to make friends with many of the others. He is always beaming and that's attractive, but he is respectful too. He listens to the other children and will offer to help them without being pushy. Sometimes he gets teased, but he doesn't retaliate as most youngsters would. He doesn't appear distressed either. I heard him say to another boy, 'Wouldn't it be dull if everyone looked exactly the same?' and I thought 'I must remember that and use it when we talk about different animals or even shapes of flowers and leaves.' We learn from the children all the time.

Q. But what can Jo do to extend Odie's social learning?

I give him responsible jobs like checking the equipment to make it ready for another child who has cerebral palsy. He fixes toys onto the slatted table and makes sure all the straps on the walking frame are in place.

We have also asked Odie to say one or two phrases in Arabic so that the other children can learn them, realise that there are other languages and respect his bilingualism. We have a Welsh child too and one who has volunteered to teach us Gaelic so we are truly learning about different ways of communicating. It's important to make all children feel they can contribute to the curriculum.

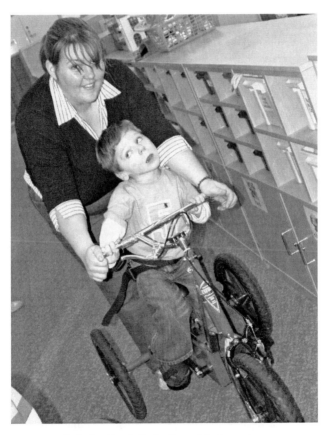

FIGURE 6.1 Jo helps Daniel's feeling of independence

97

Q. I've found that some children start off being socially strong, but soon they follow the rougher children and copy their behaviour. This is very disappointing as we try to explain the best way to behave.

At this point Dave interrupted,

> I've tried explaining what is acceptable behaviour over and over again. Sometimes giving rewards works for a short time, but often the children forget or don't seem to realise that looking out for others applies to everyone in the nursery all of the time.

He explained that chipping away at unacceptable behaviour was endlessly repetitive and totally exhausting. Pressed to give an example, he went on,

> Ben is a well-built 4-year-old who bubbles with energy. Last week on Monday and Tuesday it was so wet that the children didn't get out to play, so on Wednesday when Ben saw the bikes come out, he rushed to the door crashing the area partitions over as he went. Lia was in his way so he just pushed her as hard as he could and she fell into the box of building equipment, bruising her back. As she was marked as well as distressed we had to record the incident and tell Ben's Mum. When we did, she grabbed Ben's jersey and marched him up to Lia. 'Did he hit you?' she asked. Lia nodded shyly. 'Well, belt him back!' she was told. Lia cowered back. 'Come on, get your own back,' she went on, 'or I'll do it for you.'

The group agreed that these sorts of incidents concerned them deeply. They felt totally at a loss when home 'rules' conflicted with the caring philosophy of the early years setting. They were also aware that Ben's Mum's parting shot had been: 'Namby-pamby's no use out in the real world. That kid'll not survive if she doesn't hit back. It's a jungle out there!'

These children have to adapt to both home ways and the ways of the early years setting. 'At least in nursery, they learn there's an alternative way to behave,' claimed Dave, 'but what do we do when we get told, "My Dad says, 'If he hits you, hit him back twice as hard and he'll not do it again'"?'

This is not an easy problem to resolve, as, while the nursery can't be seen to criticise the home, the parents or caregivers have to agree that in nursery, the early years social rules must apply. Talking with the parents, calmly explaining 'this is what we do' and sending a leaflet home illustrating instances of good behaviour are useful steps. It is also a good idea to record what was done in a diary in case of later retributions. In extreme cases, e.g. when the parents or caregivers absolutely reject behaviour policies, they can be reminded that they are free to remove their child from early years care.

'Children may have been taught at home to boost their own position by rejecting those they see as being more fortunate than themselves' (Dowling 2004). Children brought up in households that are covertly, or even overtly racist, may have learned to disparage children who look different. It is in the early years that children develop a picture of who they are and if they are treated less well on grounds of their sex, or how they look or what resources they have, i.e. if they are stereotyped then their self-concept takes a devastating and longlasting blow. Practitioners have a huge responsibility in ensuring equality, i.e. making sure that all the children feel valued and respected. Of course all young children notice differences but if the practitioners can follow Jo's advice and suggest, 'Wouldn't it be dull if everyone was the same?' it might encourage children to respect differences.

ESTABLISHING EARLY YEARS 'RULES'

Q. Jo asked, 'Should we not take a much more proactive approach?'

She explained:

> When issues like this arise, we get the parents in and just tell them that we don't allow physical retaliation. Before that, of course, we would know whether a child's outburst was a one-off, or if it was his usual way of behaving. We would also have made sure we had tried to recognise any difficulties, e.g. frustration caused by poor language, that were causing the problem. But both parents and children, and all of the staff, have to show that they agree with nursery policies – it's the only way to have a stable environment.

Jo also found that some children played the staff off one against another, 'They'll hassle different members of staff till they get their own way,' she claimed. 'We have to know we are sticking to the same rules!'

Sally, whose ideal was that the children should learn to care for one another, added her thoughts. She explained:

> The reality is that the children have to learn two sets of rules, just like having one language for the playground and another for inside school. Unfortunately, many of the Playstation games and even television programmes present bullies as the stars. And the children watch them all the time. What kind of message is that?

The group nodded total agreement but felt powerless to make any change. Simon added,

> But children have always liked blood and thunder, yet they knew it wasn't real. Why should this be different now?

Debates about what encourages violent behaviour rage on.

Q. Dave was anxious to consider the layout of the nursery itself. He asked: 'Could the arrangement of the tables in the nursery contribute to rowdy behaviour? I think you have to look at the pathways around the tables and not have long runs because they encourage the children to charge around. Perhaps this is what caused Ben to lose control?'

> [Sally replied:] It's quite complicated to get the best arrangement because of access to the fire door and keeping the cooking area separate. Then there's the water tray. It's easiest if that's near the taps and the sand area can't be near the carpet. But I've just thought of a long run in our setting and I think it does encourage charging, so I'll rethink the layout and see if that helps.

HELPING THE CHILDREN UNDERSTAND SOCIAL 'RULES'

Early years staff know that, in their homes, children have different sets of rules. Indeed, some appear to have none or a set that changes from day to day or from person to person, leaving the children totally confused as to how to behave in different situations. How do practitioners begin to help them accept stability and consistency?

FIGURE 6.2 Orla and Fin work together in the garden; their interest in growing things means they are best friends

Fran explained:

> The first message we try to establish is, 'In the nursery we are all friends' and although the children can't read, we have a large notice pinned up with pictures of smiling babies, toddlers and pre-schoolers with the words underneath. Every day at one point we repeat this like a mantra! Then we discuss what a friend is. The children learn that it's someone who is kind, who lets you play and helps you with your coat. It is someone who speaks quietly and plays gently.

We let the children know we are looking out for children who behave like that and when they do we will praise them or give them a sticker. These work wonders, especially when they can take them home to show they've been good.

UNDERSTANDING AGGRESSION IN YOUNG CHILDREN

Aggression is behaviour with the intent to harm another person, and most children will show some form of aggression in the early years, possibly because they have not yet learned to appreciate what another person is feeling. In the early years, aggressive behaviour (e.g. grabbing a toy from a sibling) can be reinforced by finding that this is what works. The aggression enables the child to get the toy and this may be much more important to him than the scolding that will follow. Fortunately, aggression does tend to diminish in frequency as verbal skills improve (see Table 6.2).

Table 6.2 shows that as early as the ages of 3 or 4 dominance hierarchies come into play. Even at this early age, children understand pecking orders of leaders and followers. They know who will win a fight, which children they dare attack, and which they must avoid. This can help counter physical aggression.

At this point, the group debated the need for rewards for good behaviour, i.e. what should be the 'norm' and the conclusion was that, for a short time, rewards such as stickers, even home-made ones, were helpful for children who had to make real adjustments in their behaviour.

TABLE 6.2 Changes in patterns of aggression

Changes in the type of aggression	Children aged 2–4	Children aged 4–8
Physical aggression – e.g. biting, hitting, pushing	Most often used at this stage	Getting less
Verbal aggression – e.g. name calling, taunting	Not often used at 2; this increases as effects are recognised and language skills improve	Most often used at this age when 'rules' about hitting and biting are internalised
The reason why	Instrumental aggression aiming to procure something or to break something	The aim is to show power or to hurt feelings or humiliate another person
Why does it happen?	Frustration – often after being denied something	Competitive instinct emerging
After effects	Short lived, but bullying can emerge	Longer lasting hurt influenced by amount of support and temperament of the child

Q. I agree that stickers encourage individuals, but what could we do to explain appropriate social behaviour to a larger group? This would prevent the 'endless chipping away' (the repetition) that is so frustrating.

Fran volunteered another suggestion. She explained:

In the nursery, acting out a story with puppets is one way to show different ways of behaving. The puppets become the goodies and the baddies, and children both hear and see the results of how they behave. In one story about getting to join in a game, one puppet can be aggressive, perhaps jumping up and down shouting out 'Let me in!' while another quietly asks 'Can I play?' The first puppet is told, 'No', while the second is welcomed into the game. The children can then share their thoughts, and soon the children appreciate why some children are chosen as friends. In other words, they learn what makes children popular.

POPULAR AND REJECTED CHILDREN

Q. But why should some children be popular while others are neglected or rejected?

It is particularly important to understand these characteristics, as they seem to be relatively stable over time. Popular children are those other children choose to play with or work with, while the 'neglected' ones are tolerated without much enthusiasm. They are not actively disliked but are not sought out as friends. Sadly, the rejected ones are left isolated or openly taunted, despite the best efforts of adults urging other children to 'let them play'.

Making children aware of these characteristics could be a positive move if it enabled children to reflect and change their behaviour. While this is what education is trying to do, so many variables, e.g. the child's temperament, social background, disability and, in the early stages, physical appearance, impinge and make this change much more complex than it would appear to be at first glance. If we link these characteristics with the enduring temperamental traits explained in Chapter 1, the interaction of nature and nurture appears once more. Moreover, it is not difficult to imagine the impact on the child's self-esteem when they recognise that they are not well liked.

■ TABLE 6.3 Characteristics of popular, neglected and rejected children

Popular children tend to	Neglected children	Rejected children tend to
Be physically larger	Can't do physical tasks which others see as important, e.g. riding a bike, kicking a ball	Tell tales, complaining to adults
Be attractive, with striking physical features such as long hair	Are ordinary or average children without particular social skills; Are too clever and boastful about their own abilities	Be different in some way – even ways that are beyond their control, e.g. having physical features that others find displeasing; very over-weight children
Have a 'cool' dress sense	Lack 'street cred'	Sometimes be untidy or dirty
Behave kindly to others (crucial)	Are not consistent so other children are less sure how to communicate	Join other rejected children but with a bad grace
Be good at explaining – non-punitive	Are unsure how to fit in	Have a short fuse – will hit out or tell tales
Stay loyal to friends; consistent in the way they respond	Flit from group to group; pine to be included	Become withdrawn and/or resentful
Stay calm and rational	Are unpredictable	Be surly, unpleasant children

WHERE DOES IT ALL BEGIN? HOW DO CHILDREN DEVELOP SOCIAL SKILLS?

Ainsworth (1972), Bowlby (1988) and Robinson (2011) are key researchers into the formation and importance of attachment or bonding between parents and their children. Bowlby argues that 'the propensity to make strong emotional bonds to particular individuals is a basic component of human nature, already present in the neonate'. He shows that this early relationship is sustained by the infant being fed and by the interplay of communicative behaviours, e.g. cooing, stroking and smiling. The baby forms an attachment based on the sense of security that develops.

This research has had a profound effect on birth practices; fathers were suddenly expected to be present at the birth rather than pacing in the waiting room, so that they could share this bonding experience. Myers (1999), however, has cast doubt on the immediacy of this.

This must be a great comfort to parents whose children have had to be in intensive care or where 'the baby blues' prevented mothers from expressing warm feelings in the first days or even weeks after giving birth. The strength of the bonding is now thought to depend on the pattern of interlocking attachment behaviours that develop over the first weeks and months. As the babies and parents learn about each other they are building up a repertoire of behaviours that they know will please the other. They are fostering communication and mutuality. This is called synchrony and it takes families different lengths of time to achieve. It is fostered by cuddling, talking to the baby and encouraging/smiling at the baby's responses so that each party in the duo learns what pleases the other. A father's skills are very similar to those of the mother and so the caregivers should complement one another, allowing the baby to build two secure bonds.

But does this always happen? Sometimes parents of very premature babies are afraid to bond, fearing great distress should the baby die. Babies on ventilators and feeding tubes cannot be held, and, when they do go home, the responsibility can cause such tension and tiredness that parents can feel anguish rather than love. But usually this passes – there is time for things to settle down and for all to be well. Parents with a difficult baby, however, may feel they are underachieving, even failing, if they do not meet 'society's expectations', whatever they may be. Some parents can be disappointed in their child, especially if there is a disability, and this can be very hard to overcome. Other mothers may lack the experience of a secure and loving environment themselves; they may not have the support of the father, or enough money to cope; and, if at the end of their tether, they may abuse the child. One very young mother explained, 'I just wanted someone to love me but she didn't. She just cried all the time and in the end I hit her. I was desperate for someone to take her away and let me sleep. Yet all the time I was overwhelmed by feeling guilty too. Why did nobody tell me it would be like this?' Why indeed? Perhaps we are letting our adolescents down by not pointing out the worries of parenthood as well as the pleasures.

Happily, however, most early traumas are resolved and the attachment that is formed can last throughout life, providing mutual support for those involved. The importance of this cannot be overstated. As Schaffer (1990) claims: 'the establishment of the child's primary social relationships is the foundation on which all psychosocial behaviour is based'. He also claimed 'any early break will have long lasting effects'.

Many children have breaks of one kind or another through hospitalisation, family breakdown and going to a childminder or early years setting. Research has discovered that before 7 months old, children would settle happily with others: the children were interested rather than alarmed by their changed surroundings. But after that, the babies' responses were to cry and cling and show signs of distress. This is the classic separation effect, when children will show lengthy periods of being unsettled with their sleep patterns destroyed. The timing of bonding for the children (rather than the parents) has been judged from findings such as this.

So what happens when children go to childminders/early years setting at age 2 or 3 years? If the second setting is similar to the first and shows 'contingent responsiveness', i.e. the new caregiver responds with smiles and reassurance, then the child has a second secure base and this need not affect the attachment to the first. But where discrepancies in child-rearing practices are found, then the more vulnerable children are left with a sense of anomie, i.e. disquiet and insecurity. These findings remained constant after researchers controlled for variables such as social class. The effect of being securely or insecurely attached can last at least into adolescence. Research also found that securely attached babies became more confident youngsters; they were anxious to be involved in more activities and they had a greater sense of their own ability to accomplish things. A bonus indeed!

Melhuish (1990) compared the progress of children who experienced care with relatives, childminding or private nursery care. He found that children in early years settings received less language stimulation, possibly because of the reduced adult:child ratio. There were few differences in cognitive development but in social development the early years settings shone. The children there showed more pro-social behaviour such as sharing and co-operating with others.

SOCIAL INFLUENCES ON THE FAMILY

The specific family environment also has profound effects. The ideal environment is one where the caregivers have good interaction skills and respond appropriately to the children's cues. The children also need resources to stimulate their potential for investigating, although these need not be expensive. At the other end of the scale, some families cannot provide even the most basic comforts and the children are brought up amid chaos and despair. There are many shades of care on this continuum, so it is no surprise that children come to the early years setting with very different views of what the new experience will hold and very different ideas of what kind of behaviour will win favour or displeasure in that setting.

The family, of course, is embedded in a much larger social structure, i.e. a community, which has its own economic, social and cultural system. Infants in poor communities may be exposed to environmental toxins; they may be less likely to have immunisations and regular health care; and they may have nutritionally suspect diets. The differences in the children's backgrounds can become apparent at ages 2, 3 or 4. One remedy is to provide social support for parents in the poverty trap. Single parents may never have a break, and so as a result they are more likely to have a crying, distressed child. Providing a meeting place in the early years setting for mothers and fathers on a regular basis can mean that the children benefit from a release of the tensions brought on by isolation.

HEALTH IN THE PRE-SCHOOL YEARS

Acute illnesses such as brief bouts of sickness or streaming colds are common in the first years. Children living in more stressful settings have greater health vulnerability and this can place immense social strain on caregivers, who must make themselves absent from work in order to care for the children. The majority of accidents also occur at home and are more usual for boys than girls.

Finally for this section, Eisenberg (1990) advises us what to do if we want to rear helpful children:

1. create a warm and loving family climate;
2. explain why and give clear rules about what to do as well as what not to do;
3. provide pro-social positive feedback, e.g. 'you are such a helpful child';
4. give children opportunities to do helpful things;
5. demonstrate thoughtful and generous behaviour.

And when we read these things, we find that the early years staff group at the start of the chapter had provided a sound set of competences too.

Q. In 2013 the scourge of bullying still goes on. Despite the best efforts of most parents and practitioners, children are tormented at school. Could this be a problem in early years settings?

If the answer is 'yes' what sorts of things do they do? And if the answer is 'no', what sorts of things cause them to start? From reports of adolescent suicides, eating disorders and many unhappy children it seems that bullying is endemic across all social classes and age groups.

Q. Does it not depend on what you think bullying is?

Let's begin by reflecting on the children and the experiences they encounter. First of all, who are the children who share early years education?

They are a group of very young people of different ages (and remember that one year could mean one-third of a child's lifespan at that sort of age) and different developmental stages (some of the 3-year-olds may be more able than the 4-year-olds). They are of different shapes, sizes, colours, intellectual abilities, social competences, movement skills and emotional stabilities. Some will have the expressive language to share their needs, or will have the articulation or understanding of the nuances of language to use the spoken word – and some will not. They will have different temperaments – there are easy-going, confident and creative children, acutely anxious children, slow to warm-up children and those who will not or cannot wait. They have come from hugely varied backgrounds with different home and out-of-school experiences, different levels of common sense and different cultural beliefs. Is it any wonder that when we group all of them together in a confined space, some children, possibly attempting to gain status and make themselves heard, resort to bullying?

To add to the complexity, interest and challenge of managing these children, they are not passive learners waiting to hear the practitioners' words of wisdom and advice. They come into a new situation with different expectations of what will be there, how important it will be and what they will do to cope. Some will even recognise that people at home have expectations of them too. They have different experiences of being parented, they have learned different 'rules', e.g. whether to retaliate when they are upset, and how to do it. Some will be trained to look after resources and accept that it is their job to tidy up. Others will rebel when a non-family adult tells them what to do or decides what kinds of food they should have at snack time. The differences between home rules and early years rules can be very confusing. The children also have different levels of financial backing, home resources and support, and, to some extent, this colours their perception of their new environment.

Q. Given, then, that there are all these differences, how do children adapt to the early years setting? What things do these children have to learn?

- that they will be safe;
- how to follow a complex routine;
- how to make a friend;
- how to take turns – to wait – to deal with delayed gratification;
- how to relate to 'strange' adults and other children who may not behave the way they do;
- how to be still and listen to others;
- how to climb on a climbing frame and ride a bike outside;
- how to deal with praise and disappointment;
- how to cut out distractions and concentrate;
- how to do all the activities and tasks.

Above all, the children have to learn to respect themselves and the other children, the adults who care for them, and the resources that are provided. This takes different lengths of time depending on the willingness of the child to conform and the coherence or conflict between the child's previous experiences and this new one.

Q. I'd like to think about the setting again. Can it affect the less-confident children because they are the ones who get bullied? What can be done?

All of the intrinsic differences already mentioned are brought together in a setting which in itself may be frightening, e.g. toilets that flush noisily. (A practitioner in one setting, proud of the new self-flushing loos, was dismayed that no one would go in. It was discovered that one child had suggested a ghost was flushing them.) There are also bells that ring and radiators that buzz, walls that have too many confusing pictures, lights that flicker and doors that have double locks. 'Who needs to be kept out?' asked one fearful child. Even the large floor space can be frightening, especially if noise reverberates off the floors.

Q. How do we identify bullying behaviour?

Bullying behaviour is 'persistent, intentional, conscious cruelty, perpetrated against those who are unable to defend themselves' (Murray and Keene 1998). We would hope that not many early years age children would persist in harming the same child. But it does happen.

Q. Who are the children most likely to be bullied?

The group of practitioners made this list:

- Fragile children, e.g. small, slightly built children who don't meet the criterion of 'being big'.
- Vulnerable children, e.g. those who are different in some way: different skin colour, cultural practices, clothing or any other feature that makes the child stand out from the rest.
- Disabled children, especially those who have a hidden disability (e.g. dyspraxia, ADHD or Asperger's syndrome) because their difficulties are not immediately apparent and the children don't understand why they bump all the time or make loud noises or don't respond to their overtures in the usual way. It is interesting that often children with obvious differences, e.g. those with Down's syndrome, will be nurtured, showing that compassion can be aroused in most children. Sadly however, hurtful name-calling can affect them too.
- The most able children who know all the answers and converse in more adult ways.
- All those who can't or won't retaliate.

Q. Do you find that making children aware of the effects of bullying makes them stop?

Hopefully, pointing out the hurt that bullying causes will make all children stop and think twice about bullying behaviour, but sadly this is not guaranteed. Murray and Keene (1998) found: 'While children say they abhor the practice of bullying, many children claim it pays off, because if they intimidate others, then that stops them being bullied themselves.'

Q. Why does bullying happen?

For any reason or for no reason at all.

Q. What numbers are we talking about?

The list is frightening.

- 20 per cent of children are afraid to go to school;
- 38 per cent of primary school age children report they have been distressed to the extent that their lifestyle has been harmed;
- 15 per cent of women are affected by sexual bullying;
- 15 per cent of men are bullied at work;
- 25 per cent of adults, even old people, suffer physical and/or verbal abuse;
- 14 per cent of suicides are associated with bullying.

It can clearly be seen that bullying causes enormous hurt and damage that can last for a lifetime, or even cause a life to be extinguished. It is continual nastiness – real or even imagined, for the anticipation can be as overwhelming as the incidents themselves.

Q. Is there a gender difference? Do boys and girls use the same techniques?

See Table 6.4 for a summary of information.

The gender difference is apparent even at 4 years old. Girls are much more likely to use relational aggression (e.g. 'I'll get my Daddy onto you – he's a policeman') or bribery (e.g. 'I won't ask you to my party unless . . . '). Or they make sly faces. It is also revealing to note that girls tend to bully other girls; and they are also likely to run to an adult to complain.

Boys, on the other hand, tend to use physical aggression but, in contrast, appear to get less emotionally involved. They see bullying as par for the course, something that has to be expected and accepted. They either hit back or crumple but tend not to 'tell' until things have escalated; and of course the difficulties for both bully and victim are then more entrenched.

111

TABLE 6.4 Gender differences in bullying techniques (in per cent)

Type of behaviour	Boys	Girls
Mean to others	21.8	9.6
Physical attacks	18.1	4.4
Gets involved in many fights	30.9	9.8
Destroys things belonging to others	10.6	4.4
Destroys self/own possessions	10.7	2.1

Source: Adapted from Bee (2002).

These differences show that there are different types of bullies depending on the innate characteristics of the child, e.g. their temperament and/or the environmental/cultural experiences they have had.

Q. Does the type of bullying stay the same?

The type of behaviour used does change over time – from the overt physical abuse in the early years to the hidden, sly innuendoes later on. The variety of bullying behaviour increases, yet incidents can be difficult to describe, and can sound petty in the retelling. This is what makes it so hard for children to explain, and holds them back from sharing their fears. There is also the implicit fear that their own inadequacy may be to blame.

DIFFERENT TYPES OF BULLIES

It is important to distinguish between the different types of bullying because therein lies a clue to giving the most appropriate kind of support.

Reactive bullies

These are children who have experienced significant hurt or been overwhelmed by events either inside the early years setting/school or at home. Divorce, bereavement, even a best friend moving away may be the cause. The children lash out in frustration at their inability to remedy the situation.

Anxious bullies

These are the children who show deep-seated insecurity and they attempt to gain status through bullying. This may be a self-preservation mechanism.

Both of these need support and positive feedback. They are usually willing to listen and evaluate their actions if these are explained in a non-judgemental way.

Sadistic bullies

In contrast, there are sadistic bullies who show no regard for others' feelings. They mock any attempt to reason. They defy parents and teachers. They seem to enjoy inflicting pain. They have no altruism or empathy – they become the 'hard nut' bullies and may eventually find that only other children of like minds will tolerate them as 'friends'. In this way gangs are formed. They don't appear to care for their own well-being, or for that of others. They may have a conduct disorder, e.g. OBD (oppositional behaviour disorder) or ADHD, i.e. a neurobiological disorder requiring medical attention.

It can be hard for these children to accept that they do need help and they will usually deny that change is required. They cause resentment and many parents and teachers, after they have tried all the positive approaches, want them to be excluded from school as they disrupt learning for all the other children and may cause physical and emotional harm.

DIFFERENT KINDS OF ABUSE

The difficulty in 'sorting things out' can often lie in the fact that the type of behaviour can vary from day to day – so the 'I promise not to hide Marie's shoes again' (making her really anxious and upset) is easily kept, while at the same time another form of aggression is substituted for it.

'Not knowing what the bully will do next' can cause the victim to live in fear for the whole day.

There is also the issue that it can be the way the taunt is delivered, rather than the words themselves, that can hurt; and when these are repeated in another context, they can seem innocuous. It's often not what is said, but the way it's said, that is the problem. However, the list is endless and possibilities increase when there is less or no adult supervision. In the primary years, the playground and the area outside the school gates (where adults do not see what is going on) are often greatly feared.

PARENTS' RESPONSES

It is hugely distressing for the parents to know that their child is the victim of bullying. A first understandable reaction might be: 'What can I do? I wasn't there. I didn't see what was going on.' But others may react differently. They may:

- not know what to do and hope it will go away: 'they'll be onto someone else next week';
- brush their child's worries aside: 'I was bullied too – you just have to put up with it';
- blame the school for letting it happen: 'Wait till I get down there – they should be on top of bullying by now';
- blame their child for not coping: 'For goodness sake, wise up and stand up for yourself';
- encourage the child to retaliate: 'If he hits you, hit him back twice as hard and he won't bother you again';
- ask the bully home to see what the reaction is in the child's home setting: 'Let's see if you can be friends';
- tackle the bully themselves or tackle the bully's parents (who may or may not be aware of what is going on): 'Right, I'll sort this if no one else will';
- feel powerless, especially if there is no obvious evidence, e.g. scratches, bruises, or items being stolen.

It is not difficult to understand why parents can be confused and reluctant to act, especially if their child begs them not to interfere in case of more reprisals from the bullies, or if the staff tell them they're overreacting. Fortunately, schools have clearly laid out policies for dealing with bullying – but it still goes on.

In the early years, staff usually have more opportunities to meet the parents and build the kind of relationship that allows honest interaction.

They can confirm that the practitioners will do everything in their power to wipe out inappropriate behaviour so that each child can learn peacefully. This done, the parents can recognise that the early years setting is the very best place for their child to be and they can co-operate in eliminating aggressive behaviour.

Chapter 7

Understanding emotional development

> The emotional world of the adult influences the child and the child's emotional world will impact on the adult. Each draws a response from the other and this alters the perception of experience. (Robinson 2011)

Robinson is sure that the quality of the first attachment gives the child stability and an enduring, sound relationship that lasts across the lifespan and so influences how the child lives and learns and deals with the fun parts and the traumas that are part of everyday life. She also describes how other layers of relationships, e.g. those formed with staff in early years settings then teachers in schools can *appear* to modify the initial bonding, but 'nevertheless that first neural footprint leaves an indelible outline on the mind of the child'. Yet these second layer relationships are very strong and practitioners have to understand how influential they are in promoting long lasting attitudes and self-beliefs. Interesting too is the fact that building relationships with some children and some parents is much easier than with others. Perhaps in some duos, feelings of inadequacy or tension impact on the non-verbal cues and give inappropriate vibes to the receiver.

Or as Lewis et al. (2010) explain,

> We do not fall in love with everyone we like, nor do we become friends with everyone we meet. Instead we find characteristics in others which resonate within us, and so across a spectrum of communication and emotional empathy we become drawn to some, more distant with others and perhaps even hostile to a few.

So some children are drawn to some adults and not to others. It can be hurtful to be 'rejected' by a child but practitioners have to understand

and ensure that children do not feel rejected by them. For during the process of building a relationship, children begin to make comparisons and evaluations leading to self-evaluations and these help determine their self-concept.

Interestingly children are assessing us as we assess them.

While social skills enable children to interact with other adults and children in the early years setting in an age-related way, they are dependent on a number of emotional competences that work to let children know who they are and who others are. There is a sequence of development which is partly down to nature (e.g. the maturational unfolding of emotional competences) and partly down to nurture (e.g. the experiences and opportunities the children have and the role models which provide examples of behaviour and set cultural mores). During this process, the children begin to make comparisons and evaluations and this helps them form their self-concept. At this point Jacki said she was confused.

Q. If I think about children learning to share, then that is part of social development, isn't it? What sorts of underlying attitudes make social observations like these into emotional ones?

When we assess emotional development, we would try to discover the children's reasoning behind what they do. In the early stages, children generally have instrumental reasons for acting, e.g. 'I'd better do this because it's expected and I'll maybe get a sticker', but later if the children are developing altruism and empathy (around age 4) then the action changes: 'If I give someone this toy, it will make them happy.' This is a selfless act especially if the child would like to have the toy himself.

So when we are considering emotional development we have to pull apart the overt social acts to discover what kind of understanding is being shown. These changes are dependent on children developing a sense of self, i.e. they have to know themselves before they can appreciate the effect their actions have on others.

Q. When do children develop a sense of self? When do they have a clear picture of who they are and understand that other people have different attitudes, priorities and ideas about behaviour? How do they learn to respect different points of view? When children call out 'It's not fair', do they understand the concept of fairness, or is this just a

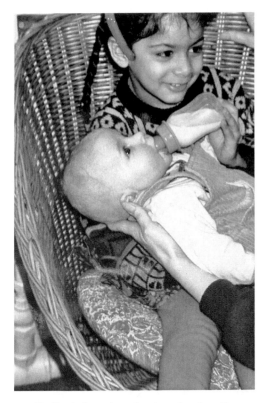

FIGURE 7.1 Sindhu is learning about caring for others and developing altruism

cry that they hope will get them what they want? And if they are fair to others who then fail to reciprocate this behaviour, what then?

These are intriguing questions that really dig deep. They add a qualitative framework to social observations because they don't look only at the things children do but they aim to find out 'why they do them', and that shows the development of these subtle qualities. And if staff record examples of children showing these qualities, e.g. when one child admires another's drawing knowing that the praise will please the recipient, staff can record this as altruism. This is an important observation, because to give and receive praise is a definite example of both generosity and confidence. Perhaps recognising altruistic acts such as these can help us

TABLE 7.1 Some emotional competences

Know their own talents and needs and accept them – while aiming to improve	Realise that other children are less able and offer them support
Be fair to everyone else	Know how to make a friend
Have enough confidence to try new things	Be ready to praise others and praise themselves too
Tell other children they are good at something	Recognise feelings, e.g. of jealousy of a new baby, and know how to overcome them
Cope with anger in an acceptable way	Have a positive self-esteem
Understand that everyone has sad thoughts and times – be compassionate to others when they are feeling upset	Be able to share worries rather than bottling them up
Recognise what another person is thinking and respect that point of view	Understand what to do to comfort someone who gets hurt

to make more of scenarios when opportunities to enhance children's emotional development arise.

The staff group were asked to put their heads together and identify some emotional competences. They produced the list shown in Table 7.1.

Table 7.1 shows a number of important developmental competences that may be hard to observe. But when should they appear? Is there an age-related developmental sequence? When does this begin?

DEVELOPING A SENSE OF SELF

Q. **You talked about a sense of self as a basis for children learning about their own selves and how they relate to others. But how do I know whether a child is developing it or not? Can I find this out when children are very young?**

In his video, 'Play for tomorrow', Trevarthen demonstrates what he calls 'an ingenious experiment' to find if children recognise who they are. This is the first sign of a developing sense of self. This involves placing a dab of rouge on a child's nose then showing him his reflection in a mirror.

The child of 3, 6, 9 and 14 months does not touch his nose because he does not know that the person he sees is himself, while the children of 2-plus do. They recognise that the reflections they see in the mirror are themselves. This is a necessary basis for making self-assessments and building comparisons between themselves and others. Many early years settings watch children enjoying their reflection in a mirror. But do they know whether they know the person there is themselves? Have they even a rudimentary sense of self? This simple test is a way to find out.

By 20 months, toddlers are beginning to understand that they are different from others. They know they have various properties, e.g. red hair, two hands and one nose. They can point to their own body parts and identify those same parts on others in picture books. This is a good way of promoting body awareness. At some time between 2 and 4 years, the children move beyond this and describe themselves by the skills they have achieved. For example, 'I can do a jigsaw'; 'I can ride a bike and tie my laces. I can paint and climb on the frame'. But these separate parts of the 'self-scheme' (or internal working model) the children have, do not yet blend into a model of self-worth. For this reason purists would not talk about early years children as having 'a self-esteem'. While they can say, 'I am good at drawing', or singing or whatever, they don't build the separate achievements into a global whole. This happens at around age 7, when children begin to make judgements about what they see as their worth. This can colour their whole attitude to new learning: 'I'm good at that so I'll have a go', or 'I'll never be able to do that so I won't try' are often-heard cries. The children are reflecting on previous experiences and transferring these assessments to new opportunities.

They are also involving themselves in deciphering how they appear to other people showing that they are developing a theory of mind. This is why it is so important that the children's first separate self-assessments are positive ones. They form the building blocks for their developing self-concept.

Q. What is the self-concept? It's a difficult term to understand. Why should some children have a more positive picture of themselves than others when they are much less able?

The self-concept is the overarching picture children have of themselves, built in the process of growing up. Particularly in the early years, the picture fluctuates as different 'important people' show different reactions. These reactions are both verbal and, even more importantly, non-verbal. The children are evaluating these reactions and so building their self-concept. If they are accurate, then there will be a match with what others see, but the child may build a false picture and that surprises onlookers.

So we can have an apparently precocious child, who considers themself to be smart and yet in reality lacks skills, and in contrast an able child who doesn't recognise their gifts at all.

It's a good idea to listen carefully to how children talk about themselves and so find what things are important to them. Pre-school children usually talk about visible characteristics, e.g. whether they are a boy or a girl, although some 4-year-olds can still be unsure of this. They will explain that they are 'big', or tell about where they live or all about their pet, i.e. concrete things, rather than whether they are brave or kind or clever, because these abstract concepts are still difficult for them to handle. They expect other people to know their pet's name and the relationships of everyone in their family photo, not appreciating that outsiders don't have the opportunities to know these things. This picture of themselves is influenced by people around them, particularly the significant others, i.e. parents, then teachers, then friends and heroes. If they are surrounded by smiling adults who have time to listen, encourage and play, then the picture is more likely to be a positive one. Even that can fluctuate when things go awry and induce self-doubt, or when illness makes the child weepy. But once these hurdles have been cleared, the positive self-concept should emerge again.

The opportunities children have to be independent and take risks influence this picture too. If children are overprotected or swamped by adults doing too much for them, they can develop 'learned helplessness', and lose the early intrinsic motivation to move and learn and cope. The self-concept picture gradually stabilises and early snapshots gradually become confirmed. This is why the early years settings have such an important part to play in determining children's long-lasting attitudes and self-beliefs.

THE EMERGING SELF-ESTEEM

Q. **Then there's the self-esteem. How does that differ from the self-concept?**

The self-esteem is the evaluative part of the picture, i.e. the self-worth. Children gradually begin to be aware that others, both family and peers, are making comparisons and judging them, even reacting to them differently according to whether they are seen to be capable or attractive or not. These evaluations (i.e. ones deduced from the tridimensional image) may be mistaken because it is so difficult to read non-verbal cues accurately. But, nonetheless, children build a picture of themselves through imagining what these judgements are. This is the self-esteem.

THE IDEAL SELF

Later, when the children begin to admire others, they begin to compare their own self to that of their ideal self. The distance they perceive between the two colours their self-esteem. It can stimulate children to strive to achieve or, if they judge the distance to be unachievable, they may give up trying altogether. This sequence mirrors the stages children pass through in their intellectual or cognitive development.

Q. How can we boost a child's self-esteem?

First of all, try to see things from the child's point of view. Most young children want to fit into their different environments and learn the kind of behaviour that is valued there. But sometimes children can find this difficult. If their names are called out time after time as people who are misbehaving, they might be hurt and withdraw, they might adopt a 'don't care' attitude, or they might ignore the correction altogether. This is why practitioners are urged to ignore minor misdemeanours as long as no other child is in danger of being hurt and to 'catch' the miscreants being good. It can be very revealing to tape a session and count just how many times one child's name is called out.

The general tenet is to give lots of praise – even for small things, as long as they are deserved. Children can usually detect false praise, but there will be something, even standing quietly, that deserves a positive mention. However, giving praise is not straightforward at all.

Giving praise

At first glance this would seem to be a simple matter of telling children they are good at something so that they build confidence in their own abilities. Unfortunately, this is not so. Children from age 3 or so are beginning to self-evaluate and make assessments for themselves. So telling them that they are proficient when they realise they're not is of little use. They recognise the truth. Certainly, children need to know that adults recognise their strengths, and fulsome praise is usually welcomed before the age when children assess their own capabilities. The move that 'all reporting home must be couched in positive terms' sprang from the realisation that negative assessments were of no use, and actually harmful. But parents know their children too. Perhaps saying what the child has achieved and then sharing a plan for development would be the best way. This could be the same for every child, the content differing for the stage of development and the individual profile of competences each child has.

A second important impact on emotional development lies in the way children are given praise. Many adults consider that public praise, when everyone stops to listen or look while the child is awarded a sticker or other reward, pleases every child. Not so. While every child likes to have their work acknowledged, many children prefer a quiet, private 'well done' or just an approving nod. They feel inhibited by public praise and may even limit their effort to avoid it.

Giving rewards

Similarly, giving rewards must be done with care. The early pleasure in gathering stickers does pass – although in the early years they still appear to be effective in promoting good behaviour. Later, however, children have their own preferences and these are the things that give most pleasure and so reinforce the child. It can be beneficial to ask the children what they would prefer rather than assume that you know. Children with autism certainly require to be asked. Sam (in Moore, 2004) chose a birthday treat of visiting launderettes to see the spinning drums and, while this is probably beyond the possibility for an early years setting, Sam's other choice of sitting on a radiator for a time might well be managed. These 'treats' would not immediately be recognised as such by those who hadn't consulted the children.

DEVELOPMENT OF THE GENDER CONCEPT AND SEX ROLES

Q. **An important part of developing a sense of self must be gender related. When do boys and girls develop this sense and what difference does it make? In the early years we try to treat boys and girls the same. Is this OK?**

Children gradually learn whether they are a boy or girl and that this state is permanent and doesn't change even when hairstyles alter or different clothes are worn. This is the gender concept. They then, through imitation and role-play, learn what behaviours are appropriate for that gender.

These are sex roles and they are very different in different cultures, e.g. how girls are valued compared with boys and what roles they are expected to play. Early years staff have to be very aware of these so that they can respect each child and don't inadvertently demean the children's cultural values and traditions. What makes this easier is the research finding that sex-role stereotypes are fairly consistent across the world. Researchers studied gender stereotypes in 28 countries and found that, even in 2004, they all described women as 'gentle, compassionate, tactful and expressive', while men were regarded as being 'competent, logical, assertive and able to get things done'. I wonder if some young children alter their behaviour, even feel pressurised to fit the mould? How stressful must this be?

Despite recent massive shifts in roles, e.g. two parents working or Dad staying home as a house-husband, 2-year-olds still appear to link Mums with vacuum cleaners and sinks. This endures even when Mums

FIGURE 7.2 Jake is enjoying the experience of being a dancer

123

are out in the workplace holding down taxing jobs. One 4-year-old insisted all doctors were men, even though his mother was one. So, understanding these stereotypes is important: they provide one mode of entry into understanding the thoughts and behaviours of young children.

These ideas complement the parts children play in different social settings. They realise that they can be leaders or helpers or take different roles such as Mum or Dad or Doctor. This can be observed as children progress through the stages of play (solitary, parallel, co-operative, then socio-dramatic). And as they develop the understanding that they are boys or girls and have this stereotypical image in their heads, they begin to assign behaviours to different roles and question, for example, whether it is right that boys should play with dolls. Six-year-olds who were asked this replied: 'Well, it's not the same kind of wrong as stealing or hitting, but it's just not right somehow. People will laugh at you if you choose the wrong things to play with.' Despite early years settings encouraging boys to dance and bake, somehow the two sexes themselves eventually allocate different preferences to each sex.

This may, of course, be reinforced at home. Even unspoken pats and smiles are strong communicators. These, plus developing interests, also explain why friendships start to be single sex, with boys choosing boys and girls, girls.

Q. When do these groups form and are there differences in the way they behave?

It's fascinating to find that as early as 3 or 4, boys and girls not only choose different toys and playmates but the patterns of interaction within the groups are different too.

Maccoby and Martin (1990) described the girls' pattern as an enabling style, which included requests, and making supportive suggestions, i.e. tactics to keep the interaction going. Boys, on the other hand, used a restrictive style. This came from observing boys trying to outwit their peers, cutting down their suggestions, e.g. 'That's sad, we're not playing that', and generally being boastful and competitive. This may explain why some children find it so difficult to sustain their participation in play activities. They may be hurt by comments that were really part of the group culture rather than being personal, but they still cause the sensitive child to withdraw.

PLAYING WITH TOYS

Q. Some children have favourite toys and will not be parted from them. Why's that? Does this show insecurity?

A great deal can be gleaned from observing the way children play with toys. It is very revealing is to see whether the toys are given a personality or are just used as familiar objects, i.e. as comforters. Often children choose the same toy, e.g. a boy choosing a truck with wheels that spin, but gradually this diminishes as the play develops. For example, the truck might become part of a game of making roads in the sand, and then possibly the game could include another truck-interested child who would build dams, or the children would include figures working or travelling on the trucks.

But another child might repeat the same action, e.g. whirling the wheels close to his ear, over and over again and resist involving anyone else. This is static play and if it endures could be the sign that obsessions are limiting the child's play.

Q. What about if the toy is a cuddly one, for example, a teddy or a toy dog?

Again, observe to see if the child gives the toy a personality. Does it have a name and does the child care for it, e.g. wrap it in a blanket and sing to it? Or is it just there, a toy with no personality, no soul?

Q. What would this mean?

Well, if this behaviour occurred with other difficulties, e.g. avoiding eye contact or not interacting sensitively with other children, then the child may have communication difficulties, for example in the way that children on the autistic spectrum do. But this needs very careful assessment before any such suggestion is made. Is the child unused to playing with others and using the toy as a shield? Has the child been ill and needs to hold the toy to show he is busy while he looks out to see what other children are doing?

MAKING A FRIEND: DEVELOPING ALTRUISM AND EMPATHY

Q. One of the most difficult things to watch is a child who doesn't get to play. Early years settings often put notices up saying 'We are all friends here', but often there's a child who can't seem to make a friend. How can we help?

Most parents' immediate hope when their children go to nursery or school is that the child will find a friend. And indeed, if they find a staunch one, then there are likely to be fewer traumas in growing up. But when this doesn't happen, children can be left out – is there anything more heart-breaking than the question, 'Why will nobody let me play?'. Sometimes, of course, the answer may be obvious, because the child is aggressive or pushy or even unkempt, but often even experienced staff can think of no reason why. So looking into the stages of developing friendships can be a first step in providing an answer.

WHEN DOES IT ALL BEGIN?

When 3-year-olds are asked, 'Who is your friend?', they will smile and offer names that may vary from day to day. But the question, 'Why do you like him?' is likely to be shrugged off or answered 'He's big' or 'I don't know'. The 'bigness' is a criterion that is beginning to permeate the child's thinking as being a desirable state, for he will have heard adults comment in admiring voices, 'Isn't he big?', but it will not mean 'big' as in offering protection or have more subtle underpinnings at this stage. The qualities very young children mention are superficial ones similar to those they use to describe themselves. It's a 'what you see is what you get' time.

But at 4 or 5 children usually have a much more enduring and comprehensive list of criteria: 'He plays with me on the bikes', 'He looks out for me and sticks up for me'. Appearance is beginning to be less important than personal qualities such as loyalty and skill even though the children may lack the language to describe what they feel.

Looking out for one another is the beginning of the development of altruism, i.e. caring for someone else even at some cost to oneself, and empathy, i.e. recognising and being sympathetic to others' feelings. This develops at about 2 or 3, i.e. at the time children begin to play with others. When children offer a toy or welcome a needy child into a game, they are showing signs that these qualities are developing. When they play, they increasingly recognise the emotions of others and respond in supportive or sympathetic ways. Often this is done by reading non-verbal cues, e.g. recognising that the child who sits with bowed shoulders and hidden eyes is anxious or sad.

DEVELOPING ALTRUISM AND EMPATHY

Eisenberg (1992) shows how important developing altruism and empathy is, for children who show more altruistic behaviour are the ones who regulate their own emotions well. They show more positive, and fewer negative, emotions when encountering new situations and are more willing to try new things. But some children can show too much altruism and overwhelm their peers. Older children have been known to steal things to pass to another child in the hope of earning friendship. This may appear to work, but the donor is likely to be rejected when he is found out or when the supplies fail to be delivered. So how can children like this be helped to find a friend?

Bee (2004) argues that it is the activity children enjoy that is the key, rather than the personality of the different children. Discovering this and pairing children so that they can discuss favourite hobbies or games is one suggestion that seems to work. Another is to discuss with the isolated children how they might get into a game. One boy waited till there was a noisy playground game and then joined in the cacophony, running and screaming as he went. He was in!

But early pro-social behaviour can change. Comforting another child, a lovely sight in the earliest years, seems to diminish in 6–10-year-olds. Younger children, even younger disadvantaged children, will donate more to others described as needy than those in older groups. Is this because they are altruistic and find pleasure in giving? Are they not so materialistic as those children with more toys and clothes, or do they not realise that giving things away means they have less? But generalities, of course, are only a part of the picture. It is interesting to note, however, that family-rearing practices can be overridden by the intrinsic intuitions of feelings developed by nature rather than nurture. The studies of adopted children show that altruistic practices tend to match the first home background better than the adopted one, even when the child has been adopted as a baby.

Q. But what about children who just won't conform? They can disrupt the whole nursery. They defy all the staff and are quite likely to hurt the other children.

This is when some physical restraint is justified in my view. Severe aggression may well be 'inherited' to some degree, and is also linked to irritable and aggressive parenting behaviour. Children may have witnessed aggressive ways of solving disputes at home and have not had guidance in using other ways. Findings like this have led to classes in child management skills.

Generally unprovoked aggression makes children unpopular, yet these rejected children try aggression to solve their difficulties, possibly because they know no other way. On the other hand, out-of-control children may have a neurological difference such as ADHD. Their neurotransmitters are providing them with too much stimulation and they are driven to run, jump and shout, even when they know that this is not the way to behave. Many earnestly try to change, but don't know how.

GROWING UP WITH SIBLINGS: THE IMPACT ON EMOTIONAL DEVELOPMENT

Q. Is it important where children come in the family? I've often heard that the middle one of three has a hard time.

Most children grow up with siblings and in the pre-school years these relationships are particularly important. Earlier research concentrated on birth order and studied the aspirations and outcomes of the first, second and third child. They found that first-borns tended to be more goal-oriented and anxious, while later children were more sociable, and more easily swayed by the opinions of others. But this was quite simplistic, because many variables, such as family income and even the sex of the other children, were complicating the picture. Newer research asks more complex questions, e.g. do parents interact differently with siblings and how does this influence the relationships they build with each other? In a longitudinal study (Bee 2002), researchers found that older siblings often began by imitating their new brother or sister, crying lustily or wanting a bottle of milk, but by the time the baby was a year old this stopped. Thereafter, the younger one copied the elder. They might show both aggression and helpful behaviours to each other. The siblings hit one another and snatched their toys, but gradually ambivalence developed as each child concentrated on their own development.

Do parents treat siblings differently? While most would deny any favouritism, the children's perceptions of this can be the basis of feelings of inadequacy and/or being second best. 'Just because my brother's in a wheelchair, we have to do everything he wants', muttered one frustrated child who obviously felt guilty at having such thoughts. But even when there are no extreme situations like that, parents can show what other children construe as favouritism, although they may deny such a charge.

CASE STUDY

Jake was a sensitive, gentle boy. His sister Grace was a tomboy, always in scrapes. Now although her mother appeared to admonish her, the tone she used, 'What a rascal you are', was complimentary, making Jake feel he was inadequate. He wished he could be a tomboy too. Over a period of time the resentment built up, and, especially when copying his sister, he in turn behaved badly. That was different. His act was seen to be malicious rather than naughty, and there were no hardly hidden smiles to soften the blow. No one recognised that Jake was trying to find ways to be on a par with his sister. He became an unhappy, withdrawn little boy.

So subtleties in child-rearing practices abound and the children soon learn to evaluate them. These can affect their emotional state, either building or knocking their confidence. Many children try to change, as the picture they have of themselves doesn't please them – but most often they don't know how. It is when frustration boils over that adults see the results of poor child-rearing skills.

ETHNIC AWARENESS, IDENTITY AND PREJUDICE

Ethnic awareness

Q. **I remember having a little African girl in my nursery. All the other children were fair skinned and wouldn't have met a child from Africa before, yet they gave no sign of noticing any difference? When does this develop?**

As children grow they become aware of differences in hair and skin colour and in facial appearance and body-build, i.e. differences due to ethnic origin. By age 4 or 5 children will recognise basic distinctions and by age 8 or 9 they realise that these are permanent, despite superficial changes in attire.

129

Ethnic identity

This is awareness of one's own ethnicity. It is usually assessed by asking children to look at pictures of dolls and to point out which one is like them. However, a child might be swayed by a kind facial expression or a preference for the clothes the dolls wear, so it is important to test this using several dolls and/or on different occasions. Children need to know who they are and to be proud of belonging to their cultural heritage. In 2006 children from impoverished parts of Namibia were taken to other regions to appreciate the scenery and the wildlife and so develop national pride. Experiences like this helped them to appreciate their culture and their country. Early years settings here are trying to follow this by embracing different cultural practices and demonstrating to all children that differences enrich lives.

Ethnic prejudice

Q. When does prejudice begin?

It can be difficult to separate out ethnic preference from prejudice unless it is an overt act. Children at 4 may prefer to play with their own ethnic group without attributing any negative overtones to those in the other group. In cases of preference, when children from different ethnic backgrounds do play together, there would be no change in their behaviour. On the other hand, prejudice implies a negative evaluation of another person on the basis of sex, disability or race. Largely absent at age 3 and 4, this develops at age 5 or 6, when children begin to see others as being different and they tend to link negative assessments with this. In his film *Child of Our Time* (2006), Robert Winston showed young children from a minority group pointing out pictures of people they would like to play with. In the main, these were children in the majority group. This was so sad, and shows how much work is still to be done.

Q. What do early years settings do to combat this?

Most practitioners now try to understand the backgrounds and religions of all the children in their care and they celebrate the important festivals and special days of all the groups so that the children's learning is extended in positive ways. Divali has a place in the curriculum just like Christmas and the Chinese New Year, and the children share all the exciting, very

FIGURE 7.3 Making bagpipes adds to the fun in celebrating Burns'
Night

different things. Parents come into the the early years setting to bake
traditional dishes with the children, and they show traditional costumes,
e.g. kilts and saris, or share making artefacts such as Chinese lanterns or
dragons. Working together in groups like this can improve inter-racial
respect.

This cultural richness is very important. Children have only one
childhood, and early years staff must try to make sense of all the complex
understandings and relationships that make children what they are.
Practitioners are often nervous of being seen to favour one child and can
only be vigilant about treating each child with respect and giving each
one a fair share of teaching and listening time. This is not an easy thing
to do.

Chapter 8

Understanding moral development

As children mature and become more independent, they are expected to make moral judgements about what is right and what is wrong. This usually involves them in following the prevailing, accepted, cultural 'rules' of right and wrong. Often these are internalised, the children observing their parents rather than having explicit explanations of these rules. And some groups will live by different rules to others. Surely we all need rules if society is not to be chaotic? But when children act according to these rules, are they making moral judgements or are they only following a code that will ensure they are praised or rewarded for so doing? Can we/should we/how should we teach children to be 'good'? Is there a fine line between co-operation, conformity and coercion?

Play is the focus of the early years curriculum. It is a child's world, a time when children develop understandings and learn the skills they need to cope as they become more independent. Surely then, adults should be helping children learn appropriate behaviour as they play? There have been many authors who have resisted adults' attempts to do just that, considering intervention morally reprehensible. Cohen (1990) was one such. He was adamant that adults should not intervene in children's play.

'How can we, long out of practice oldies teach children how to play?' he asked. He continued: 'and when I hear of adults saying things like "at play the children should learn to take turns and share things," I have to ask, "Are there social engineers on the swings?"' He considered that any intervention removed both freedom and ownership from the children.

'Some children,' he explained, 'mistakenly thinking adults know better, will acquiesce, but then they wait for adults to tell them what to do.' He claims that such intervention denies children the opportunity to be creative and imaginative. 'Some will rebel,' he adds. 'I hope they do!'

As a dancer many years ago, I was taught that I had to learn the movement technique first, and only when these skills were learned could I use them to be expressive. The technique was the foundation that guaranteed safety (from injury) and survival (employment). So dances that were known to 'be good' were taught until the technique was mastered. But then another teacher explained, 'From the start, all technique should be expressive, so that you can be creative and make the dance your own.' The trouble was that many of the dancers, unused to such freedom, could not use it. They had not developed the creative side of their thinking when they were mastering the technique. Creativity didn't happen as a natural follow-on after all. Of course, no one had explained this progression, i.e. that this was what was supposed to happen, either. Does this analogy match teaching in the early years? Is there a way to pass on the techniques without stultifying imagination? Will this make intervening in children's play 'right?'

Q. So, in the early years, how do children develop a sense of what is right or wrong? Where do they get this information?

Perhaps in a chapter on morality, it is best to answer by posing more questions. For example, are the many instances of things 'one just doesn't do' explained to children, or are these constraints context-bound? They learn that it's 'naughty' to barge around the early years setting shouting and letting off steam, but in the park, that's perfectly all right. And when a child tells another 'you're fat'— when the child is fat – is that wrong? Hurtful statements are not socially acceptable, but adults can worry in private about a child's obesity, keeping the concern from the child; or they may consider the weight is puppy fat and it will disappear in its own time. But they may be denying the child the chance to do something about it. Who is 'right'?

Most children are expected to absorb this moral sense from the role-models around them, and, of course, these people may have a very different code from the one(s) taught in schools. Some parents may scorn people who work. Some regard the early years setting and school as free childminding, not education at all, while others want to push their young children into inappropriate formal learning. Another group is happy to leave education to the staff, either because of a laissez-faire attitude or because they genuinely believe that the staff are professionals who know best. These different stances are absorbed by the children and must affect their perceptions of what is right and wrong and, particularly for older children, how they value their time in school. In turn this affects their behaviour.

Some parents may have given a great deal of thought to the moral well-being of their children, but at times of stress, fatigue and even love, may understandably lack the time or energy they need to stand by their principles. So the children receive mixed messages. And if the parents disagree on what their child should be allowed to do and say, what then? The children soon learn to play one off against the other. But is this only the parents' dilemma? How often have we asked children in the early years setting to do as we say rather than copy what we do?

Other parents believe that any repression will mar a child's free spirit and that their children will successfully make their own moral code for themselves. They believe that total freedom of choice is essential before children can be said to be making moral judgements. The different groups are passing on very different lifestyle messages to their children. Furthermore, these children, in another setting, may be judged for following the way things are done or not done at home.

Q. How do children learn to make judgements about what is right and wrong?

This is a huge topic. The most reported researchers in this area are Kohlberg (1969) and Piaget (1932). Piaget claimed that, in their early years, children were bound by concrete findings, i.e. what they could see and hear. They were not attuned to abstract competences such as recognising intention. So he devised an experiment to test this theory. His experiment aimed to show whether children took intention into account when making judgements about right or wrong and when giving punishment for an act. When would children see intention as a contributory factor to the outcome and so affect their judgement of what was done? Piaget told a group of children two short stories, then asked them their thoughts.

Story 1
A little boy called John was in his room when he was called down to dinner. He went into the kitchen where the meal was to be, but behind the door was a tray with 15 cups. John didn't know that the cups were there, but when he knocked them over, they all broke.

Story 2

One day when his Mum was out, a little boy called Henry climbed up on a chair to get some jam from a cupboard. He couldn't reach it, but as he stretched up, he slipped and broke a cup that was on the shelf.

The children were asked 'which child was the naughtiest?'. Do you think it was John or was it Henry?

The 5-year-olds found that 'both children were naughty' but when it came to the question of punishment, then the boy that broke 15 cups was thought to deserve 'more slaps' (Jack aged 5). They were only concerned by the outcome, i.e. the amount of damage, and did not consider the intention, i.e. that John could not have known the cups were there and so could not have prevented the accident. Teegan, aged 7, however, claimed that Henry 'knew he was doing wrong – he did it on purpose and he should be smacked'. In contrast, 'John had an accident,' she explained. 'He didn't know the cups were there.' 'Who put them in that silly place?' asked Gail, aged 9. She had a much more sophisticated conception of events and was anxious to follow the story to a logical conclusion by finding the real culprit.

In line with Piaget's work on conservation, later researchers claimed that explanations or more child-friendly language could help children to develop awareness of intention at an earlier age. However, Piaget was looking for implicit understandings, i.e. what children brought to a situation, not what they could do after teaching. So responses depend at least to some extent on how children are brought up, e.g. whether they are taught to consider scenarios as problem-solving events and whether they are ever encouraged to justify their thoughts and actions.

Q. When we talk about how children should be brought up, we probably think back to our own experiences and try to extract the good parts and avoid the mistakes (in our retrospective view) our own families made. But each of us has only one life experience and that may be very different from the one another person has. How are we to know what else goes on, and what the implications are for children brought up with different sets of standards?

Styles of parenting are very different. Let's look at the work of Maccoby and Martin (1990) who describe four types.

135

AUTHORITARIAN PARENTS

Authoritarian parents insist on high levels of control, but show little warmth or responsiveness to their children. They are there to be seen and not heard. Children from these families are used to being told what to do with little room for manoeuvre. They hear the instruction 'do this' or 'don't do that' with no explanation as to why and no leeway allowed. The parents may consider that strict discipline encourages high standards. So, in the early years setting, in a less restrictive atmosphere where commands are replaced by requests, children may be confused and unable to make decisions or imagine the implications of their actions. On the other hand, they may revel in the freedom and become loud, aggressive and out of control. Parents who smack to get obedience are most often in this authoritarian group.

PERMISSIVE PARENTS

The permissive style is high in nurturing, but low in maturity demands, control and communication. Children brought up in this way can enjoy a great deal of freedom, but lack guidance and do not know how to behave appropriately in different settings when they can't do as they please. Indulgent or over-permissive parents may find that their children show signs of aggression too. These can surface when the children have to do as they are told. The children are less likely to want to take responsibility and may do less well in school.

AUTHORITATIVE PARENTS

This pattern has been shown to produce the most reliable, self-confident children. The parents are in control and respond to the children's needs so that they feel secure, yet the children know they can ask questions and receive considered explanations. Dowling (2004) explains that such loving support 'helps the "right" behaviour to stem from a basis of understanding', and she claims 'children in this kind of relationship with their parents, will want to behave in a way that pleases them'. But perhaps this fluctuates as other people, e.g. the peer group, replace the parents and the teachers as the most 'significant others' in children's lives?

NEGLECTING PARENTS

Children who are subject to this pattern are most likely to be aggressive and hostile. This can be down to the psychological unavailability of the parents. They may be depressed or ill or bored by the difficulties of bringing up children and 'escape' mentally or even physically. The children in turn are likely to show great difficulties in forming relationships and, when older, they are likely to attach to antisocial groups made up of other neglected or rejected children, who may be the only ones who empathise with this kind of behaviour.

MORAL REASONING AND MORAL BEHAVIOUR

Q. So how can early years practitioners come to understand the intricacies of moral development when the children in their care have come from a myriad of family and community backgrounds?

There are two aspects of moral development that are interdependent, but the complexity comes in that one does not always follow the other.

The first is moral reasoning, i.e. how we judge whether an action is right or wrong; the second is moral behaviour, which doesn't always follow. The first is about knowing, and the second, doing. For example, a child may know it's wrong to steal someone else's sweets, but the temptation can be too strong and the deed is done anyway. Whether feelings of guilt follow or whether the child justifies (to themselves) their action, e.g. 'Well, I am never allowed sweets and he has them all the time', depends on their stage of moral reasoning and the influence of their home environment. If the child has been brought up to take what they want, then their perspective on what they have done will be different to that of a child who knows their parents will not approve – but that child may take the sweets nonetheless. On the other hand, the second child may act correctly and deny themselves the treat, but feel frustrated by being constrained by their conscience.

The reactions of parents can be hugely different too, as the following extreme examples will show. Smith, Blades and Cowie (2002) cite the examples of two sets of parents whose children were killed by other children. The first was the toddler Jamie Bulger, killed in the UK by two 10-year-olds, and the second was a 6-year-old child, Silje, in Norway. The public described Jamie's killers as 'evil' and the outcry made it clear that long prison sentences should be the punishment. But in Norway Silje's mother found she could not hate the three young boys who did the dreadful deed. This was 'because they were children'. These very different responses reflect very different thoughts on when children should be held morally responsible for their actions. Would the forgiving response help the parents cope and allow them to move forward? Was this better (for them), than the fear that engulfed parents in the UK and led to some playgrounds being encased in wire fences and children at home 'not being allowed out to play'? There are no easy answers to questions like this, except that moral judgements must be made in the context of the family and community to which the child belongs.

When do these dilemmas begin? If children come from a poverty-stricken home with no moral guidance, should they be expected to behave and be treated differently?

CASE STUDY

Carly tells of her experience:

> Well, we had tried just about everything to make Josh behave. He's a bright boy who seeks attention all the time. The trouble was that the other children knew he was the naughty one and they goaded him to misbehave and enjoyed him getting scolded. He didn't seem to mind; in fact he just shrugged and looked as if he was enjoying the attention, so scolding didn't do any good. We were advised to note how often his name was called out and do it less, so we tried that; we even tried to ignore bad behaviour that didn't hurt any of the other children, but that had little effect as well. So the next move was to give him responsibility and let him know he was important. 'Josh, we have chosen you to check that the story sacks have all the books and toys,' we said. Immediately there was an outcry. 'I wanted to do that and I've been good all day,' cried Alana, 'why does he get to do it when he's a bad boy?'

How can staff explain to children that the punishment doesn't always fit the crime? Will any of these techniques work when children are so young? At what age can any child be thought to be morally responsible? These are difficult questions. Thankfully, even in severely disadvantaged homes where the children have had to learn survival skills and become streetwise early, most children will not harm others, at least not severely. But many have to have repeated explanations of what is acceptable behaviour and some have to be restrained, even excluded, if their behaviour threatens others. And even at this early age, some children bully others, and steal or spoil their work, apparently without thought, even appearing to gain pleasure by their malicious acts. Yet others, no matter what their apparent disadvantages, are very caring and share what little they have with no thought for themselves.

DISCUSSION TOPIC

Kay is a medical student and during her holiday she went to a shelter for children with HIV in Africa. In material terms these children had nothing, yet they could enjoy a game with one burst ball, kicking it happily in the sand. All the children played; there was no 'choosing teams' and leaving one child last. These children just joined in without worrying about being picked; there were no rules and when goals were scored between two canes stuck into the sand, everyone clapped.

When Kay said to one little boy, 'what a nice T-shirt you are wearing,' his immediate response was to try to take it off. 'You must have it, for I love you,' was his response. This was the only T-shirt he had.

Kay explained how humble she felt, and she became determined to raise funds to send toys to the children. But would these toys introduce the idea that material things were more important? Would all the children still smile?

What is the best way forward?

If children are to develop moral reasoning for themselves and gradually build a value base, they must be able to think through various courses of action and make decisions about what to do and how to do it. They must be able to anticipate the consequences of their behaviour. How much harder must that be if the children have not had any consistent reactions to the behaviour at home.

Q. How does the age of children influence what they do?

From his research into how children came to resolve moral dilemmas, Piaget (1932) distinguished three age-related stages. He claimed that up to age 4 or 5, the rules of a game or rules at play were not understood;

in the second stage the rules were seen as coming from a higher authority (God, adults, teachers) and could not be changed. The third stage at 9 or 10 years saw the children negotiating rules and changing them if everyone in the group agreed.

Piaget's stages have been criticised (the language in some tests was not child-friendly but once that had been changed the children achieved more at an earlier age; and other researchers replicating the tests have similarly found that with explanations children could show achievement at earlier ages), but he was the first to set a stage or maturational theory – he was not talking about how children reacted to teaching, and children long ago had very different upbringings to those they have now (my thoughts). Despite these criticisms his work has stayed as of immense importance for parents and teachers learning about how children develop.

So, at age 4 or 5, children may learn rules about behaviour in an instrumental way; they may accept them, rather like learning by rote, without realising or asking 'why?' They may pull away in frustration when they are thwarted, yet not be able to offer an acceptable alternative. They may have several sets of rules for different settings and obey or reject them on different days. Only when they reach the age of being able to weigh up implications and act accordingly can they be said to make moral judgements on their own.

Q. This would seem to suggest that it doesn't matter what children do? Surely this can't be right?

Of course it's not! This is the time when the children absorb values and learn about co-operation and sharing and trusting. At this critical time, when the children are learning faster than at any other time, role-models can help them understand morally sound ways that, we hope, will stand them in good stead in the future, no matter what slings and arrows they meet.

Two traumatic events are separation of the parents and the death of a close relative or a much-loved pet. How can staff support young children when these unhappy events intrude in their young lives, before they can foresee the implications of each, and when their parents are also distraught?

Q. It must be terrible for children when their parents separate. What kind of reactions should we expect?

Any conflict between parents can be very distressing for children who then have divided loyalties. When this is the norm, anxieties pervade their childhood and translate into their having more difficulty in sustaining friendships and focusing on their work in school (Katz and Gottman 1993). And when disagreements and arguments lead to separation, this is not usually an immediate decision. Unhappiness and anxiety will have begun long before that time. Awareness of the effects of warring parents on their children needs to be recognised well before separation or divorce occurs.

When separation does happen, Davies and Cummings (1994) found that in their research group (made up of children of age 4 and 5), these same children were still traumatised at 9 years old. Their teachers reported them as showing much more antisocial behaviour than occurred in groups of other children of the same age and of similar social status. So effects of separation on children can be profound and long-lasting.

The effects have been found to vary according to the ages of the affected children, with the youngest groups less affected because they are less aware of the implications that accompany divorce. They may not realise that such a decision will not be revoked, thinking that the absent parent will come home at a later date. When this doesn't happen, they may decide that they have caused the split and be consumed by guilt. Although irrational, this is nonetheless very painful for the child, especially if the child cannot confide in or be reassured by the parent who is still there.

The material deficits resulting from divorce are likely to cause hardship too. Moving home may be necessary and, for the first time, money may be short and a topic of wrangling between parents. A non-working parent may have to get a job and the split may mean that one set of grandparents, who might have helped out with childminding or even financially, lose contact or feel alienated, causing more grief all round. In the extreme, children may be abused if they are thought to have caused the disharmony. This can happen if parents conceive of relationships in terms of power struggles so that they are constantly tense. Studies show that children with step-parents may be abused too. Why should this be? It could be that it is not in a step-parent's genetic make up to invest in children who are not related. While most step-parents make huge efforts to be accepted and are often successful, some of the strategies they try are not able to work because the new members of the family are seen (by the children and possibly the grandparents) as intruders, even as the cause of a close relation being ousted from the family group.

It is not easy to see how the early years setting can help, beyond giving the children time to talk and reassuring them that the early years setting will stay the same. Of course, allowances have to be made, but practitioners are often at a loss what to say. What advice is given? How can the effects be minimalised and the consequences reduced? Several pieces of advice for parents, carers and teachers taken from different research reports are listed below. They are:

- Keep the children in the same environment; keep changes to routine to a minimum, and provide familiar activities and experiences to give the children security.
- Parents who retain the main role are advised to try to maintain a quality of life for themselves, e.g. to continue with activities that were enjoyed before the separation. Keeping up a wide circle of friendships has positive results; one very important result being that the children don't become isolated.
- Practitioners are advised to listen to the child, but not to take sides. They have to remember that the child may be biased by not appreciating all the ins and outs of the situation. Moreover, if the practitioner blames a parent, the children are likely to want to defend him or her, regardless of where they themselves might allocate blame. Practitioners are urged to stay in contact with the remaining parent, staying positive and not breaching the child's confidence. Any suspicion that this has occurred will destroy any trust in the relationship, which at this stage might at least partially compensate for the one lost at home.

Many of these strategies depend on getting to know the individual children and family as well as the community context in which they are placed. The early years setting is the place to start building relationships, and staff there should be given the time to get to grips with these complex issues, for separation and/or divorce impact on nearly every child, either directly or as a friend.

COPING WITH BEREAVEMENT

Q. **How do practitioners in the early years support children who are experiencing bereavement?**

Again, it's a question of understanding each family's perspective, gauging how much the child wants to know, and finding what the children are likely to ask (from the literature or experienced teachers).

Q. What do children think when a friend or a pet dies?

Adults know that death is irreversible, that it comes to everyone, and that families are usually very sad. Young children have a different set of beliefs. Bee (2002) explains: 'Pre-school children believe that death can be reversed, through magic or prayer or wishful thinking' or even, perhaps, like the princess in the story book, by a kiss from a prince. They also believe that the members of their own family can avoid death.

Many believe that 'children can't die – you have to be really old and ill'. This can stand children with terminal or life-threatening illnesses in good stead. 'If I take my medicine, I'll go back to school next term,' explained one 5-year-old who was slowly losing the battle with cancer.

Understanding this stance, i.e. don't burden the children with more detail than they request, will inhibit lengthy explanations that may only serve to confuse the children. It will be vital to discuss with the family how they want the early years staff to talk with the child. Some disparate views show the controversy here. 'Don't mention Granny dying at all,' said one Mum, 'for when he's at nursery I want him to be able to forget all the sadness that's at home.' 'I think how you dealt with the hamster dying, burying it and making a special song and having a little ceremony, helped Charlie understand,' said another Mum. 'She learned it was OK to be sad and that it was good to keep talking; she knew she could ask questions but it was awful when she asked where the hamster had gone and when it would come back. I wished we were religious because that would give us some comfort' (Collins 2005).

Different cultures regard death quite differently. In some North American cultures, children learn that death is a time for composure and dignity. It is talked of as 'part of nature's natural cycle' and as such it is not feared. In Mexico, death is celebrated, they even have a 'Day of the Dead' in the midst of their festivals.

In the UK today there is much more talk of celebrating the person's life than mourning those who have died. But, of course, it may take time for the reality and the rhetoric to blend. Meantime, in the early years setting, practitioners have to listen to and support the child, and often this extends to the adult members of the families as well.

143

Chapter 9

Understanding intellectual development

While most professionals and parents value all aspects of their children's development and come to understand how the interplay of each contributes to learning, many tend to see the social, emotional, moral and motor contributions as underpinnings of the intellectual one. This may well depend on what they see as the purpose of education in early years settings and schools. They may have an instrumental view of education and see its purpose as providing the children with the skills to get a job that, in turn, allows them to achieve a good standard of living, in which case they are likely to view mathematics and literacy skills as the most important. On the other hand, some may take a broader view and want their children to be creative and imaginative, enabling them to appreciate the 'good things' around them. This is an expressive or aesthetic stance. They will be anxious that music, drama, art and movement are given prime time.

But of course, the two ways of thinking are not mutually exclusive. Professionals in the early years, appreciating the intellectual learning potential in both these stances, strive to provide a balance that includes all the topics in a play-based curriculum.

Once again practitioners were asked taxing questions.

Q. **When you focus on intellectual development, what are the skills and competences that you want your children to be able to know or do?**

- Basic counting (i.e. numbers 1–5). For example, the number of children at the water tray; the number of buns in a baker's shop.
- Know their colours – at least the primary ones. The 4-year-olds learn about mixing colours and how they change to make

FIGURE 9.1 Learning can be a multi-sensory experience

FIGURE 9.2 Singing and playing percussion helps rhythm and timing as well as providing lots of fun

others. They learn more subtle shades, e.g. lilac, at appropriate times (for example, when the tree blossoms).

- Make circles and patterns (i.e. emergent writing). For example, some children will want to write their name, while others will want to learn to control a pencil or paintbrush.
- Listen to a story and remember/anticipate the sequence (for example, in 'The Three Little Pigs').
- Clap out the rhythm of jingles and nursery rhymes.
- Be able to follow a routine and to become more independent.
- Remember things without always having to ask.
- Stay focused on a task for some time (for example, arrange beads in sizes or colours then thread them). The children need to be aware of the pattern they are creating.
- Show respect for other cultures (for example, festivals, foods, ways of dressing) and for other children.
- Know how to look after the environment (for example, through helping in the garden and appreciating the activities of the wildlife). Indoors, realise that tidying and recycling are important.
- Understand the foods children should choose to keep themselves healthy. Enjoy them at snack time.
- Recognise their names and the sounds of a few individual letters such as 's' and 't'.
- Be able to remember a message for their parents.
- Know who is fetching them and get ready independently.
- Be able to role-play in the different areas, for example, be a nurse in the hospital corner or a fire-engine driver.

These descriptions of what the children should know or be able to do over the two years in the early years setting do sound as if the content of the curriculum is decided in advance and is taught according to a set of predetermined criteria. But while these targets certainly guide planning, again balance comes into play. This time it is a balance between pre-set curricular goals (the timing of the introduction of those goals and the children's readiness to absorb and interact with materials and experiences) and allowing the children to make decisions about the topic they wish to study. And, as children develop at different rates and learn best in different ways, as well as come to the early years setting from widely differing backgrounds, decisions about when and how to introduce new learning are part of the discussions the team will hold every day. To be totally appropriate for this age group of children, the early years curriculum has to be based on developing learning through play.

Q. So there are a number of questions to be answered before we make plans?

Important questions would be:

- What do children coming to the early years setting already know?
- What skills are already developing?
- What learning experiences will allow children to fulfil their potential while achieving the competences or targets in the guidelines/curriculum documentation?
- Are there ways that transfer of learning can be highlighted/explained?
- In what ways are the children developing competence in the activities of daily living e.g. having opportunities to organise resources/their own personal belongings?

LEARNING LANGUAGE

Q. What are the early signs of developing language?

As early as 1 or 2 months babies gurgle and make cooing sounds. Sometimes they can be heard trying these sounds at different levels and pitches and chortling with pleasure as they do. Between 9 and 12 months this develops into monosyllabic babbling – repetition of the same syllable, e.g. 'dadadada' or 'mamamama'. Naturally, parents are charmed by this early form of communication, which is really practice for the next stage, 'jargon' (often called variegated babbling). In jargon, babies string together different syllables with intonations that sound like sentences. Often adults repeat these back to the baby as a game and this is the basis of turn-taking in language development. If turn-taking is difficult for 3-year-olds, playing games like peek-a-boo can instil the 'speak then wait and listen' idea.

Non-verbal communication

Of course, children don't depend on vocals to make their needs known. Non-verbal communication conveys most – some would claim 90 per cent – of the meaning in a message. Think of the baby stretching out towards a favourite toy. The actions of clasping and unclasping a hand and possibly grizzling as an accompaniment, leave no doubt as to the child's wish. So babies can communicate their wishes long before they can talk.

Understanding language

Q. **But when do babies really understand the words that they hear?**

Receptive language, which is the name given to the understanding that precedes the expressive language stage, begins at about 9 or 10 months, and by 12 months the babies should understand about 30 words. By 13 months, though, the understanding rises to about 130 words – a large increase. So although they do not speak, babies are learning all about the sounds and the intonations of their language and they benefit from being exposed to a rich variety of words.

Emergence of the first words

First words generally appear at about 12–13 months. These may be made-up words rather than recognised words. Until about 18 months these are single words. Toddlers often combine a word with a gesture to clarify what they mean. They might point to a pair of shoes and say only 'Daddy's' when they mean 'There are Daddy's shoes'. This shows that their comprehension is much more developed than their articulation.

It is so interesting to find that deaf babies of deaf parents go through the same first stages in their language development at the same rate. At about 12 months they will make a sign, e.g. raising an imaginary cup to their lips to indicate they are thirsty. And hearing children of deaf parents still speak at the same time as if they had been born into families without disability. Yet they have probably been exposed to much less verbal interaction.

When the language spurt occurs at around 18 months, most of the words children volunteer are 'naming words', e.g. 'doggie', 'car', 'hat' and so on. A smaller number use an expressive style. Their earliest sentences are linked to social relationships using prepositions, 'I want Mum' rather than naming objects. The expressive style sounds more advanced than the naming or referential style but they are really only different ways of thinking. This reminds observers to look for individual differences when they identify developmental norms.

Q. From what you've said, it would be important to read stories to babies, even when the words seem rather hard?

'Reading together' is important from the earliest days because the children are learning that the words on the page are the sounds that are heard. At 9 months or so the baby can begin pointing to objects and naming them or querying what they are called. More expressive babies will want you to explain, 'This is the little girl's doll', i.e. explaining social relationships rather than building a vocabulary of nouns.

Q. I've heard of 'Motherese'. What's that?

'Motherese' or, as it is now called, 'infant-directed language', is the simply constructed repetitive language mothers use to communicate with their babies. Parents tend to speak to their babies using a higher pitch and this appears to intrigue the baby and keep it listening. So simple sentences are internalised through repetition and imitation.

Talking in sentences

By 30 months infants have a vocabulary of about 600 words and by 5 years children have 15,000 words, an increase of 15 new words a day (Pinker 1994). First sentences are short – often described as 'telegraphic speech'. But gradually, inflections are added, along with prepositions, plurals and past tenses, such as 'I wented to nursery'. These '-ed' additions, which are gradually lost, stand out and endorse the claim that children make up their own language structure even when they have not heard such usages before.

As the pre-schoolers gather a huge number of names for things, they go through a time called 'naming explosion' when they point and constantly ask to know what things are called. This precedes the ability to categorise or group objects – the first sign of mathematical learning.

Although language acquisition is not yet fully understood, the fact that children acquire a 'complex and varied use of their language within a few years is nothing short of miraculous' (Bee 2002). And when we hear 3-year-olds explaining, cajoling and demanding, we can only agree.

Q. What about the development of mathematical thinking? Sometimes even 3-year-olds will chant numbers up to 10 or even 20.

At this stage the children are usually simply regurgitating what they have been encouraged to learn by rote. They are enjoying the sound of numbers – and this is a good thing – but it doesn't mean they have any real understanding of what they're saying. Children have to learn to count objects, giving each a number, and this can be very hard. Their naming skills suddenly disappear and the trail is lost. This is why early years settings start by explaining that they should, for example, choose two items at snack time, or check that three people are at the water tray. They are then seeing the numbers in action. Many number songs are great favourites and they instil the importance of numbers as well.

Some researchers advise that young children should work with small numbers and learn to count forwards 1 to 5 and backwards 5 to 1. If they assign each number to a sequence of blocks or cars, i.e. concrete objects, then they come to understand the basis of addition and subtraction. A good test of understanding is to put out 5 clothes pegs or small toys and ask the child, 'Please give me two'.

Q. But maths is more than number work isn't it? What other sorts of activities help children's mathematical development?

Many activities develop mathematical understanding, for example: filling an egg box with small objects is visually reinforcing the number 6, estimating how many apples will fill a basket is an introduction to capacity, while different-sized jugs ready to pour water help an understanding of volume. Recognising shapes such as circles and squares leads to an appreciation of two-dimensional shapes, and later three-dimensional ones; and even colouring-in requires some thinking about directions and stresses, i.e. mathematical concepts. In fact, analysing any of the early years activities will reveal some mathematical learning. Siphoning water when at the water tray area, and finding how to make the fluid travel quickly and slowly, measuring and weighing at the baking table, giving out one apron to each child at the craft table – all of these are subtle ways of introducing the concept of numbers.

Mathematical language develops as the children experience a range of activities and listen to instructions such as 'Pour in more water', 'How many spoons do we need?', 'Make the ball stop inside the circle', 'Thread the needle through the bead', and so on. Comparisons are also fun and lead to mathematical understanding, e.g. in an activity involving rolling plasticine to strengthen fingers, questions such as 'Who made a long thin snake and who made a short fat one?' will encourage the children to recognise lengths and widths and recognise that the same size ball of plasticine can make different shapes.

Q. All of these involve the children in doing things/handling materials. Is this what's meant by concrete learning?

The children need to see and handle objects if they are to understand the effects of manipulating them. Young children live in the present and cannot readily visualise what is not in front of them. Abstract thinking, i.e. envisaging things not present, is a much more sophisticated mode of thinking. The possibilities of mathematical computation increase as this is achieved. But in the early years setting, because most children are visual learners, handling, doing and seeing are the most effective learning strategies.

CHANGING CAPACITIES IN THINKING

It is when children are about 3 years old that they begin to use one object as something else, e.g. a yo-yo becomes a toy dog. This is the development of the use of symbols, and can be readily seen when observing children at play.

Q. Play moves through developmental phases as the children begin to use symbolism. They become less tied to the here-and-now, and can imagine events that might happen, or, for example, remember going to Grandma's some time ago. What are these stages?

The word 'stages' is not used so much now, due to the realisation that there are rarely abrupt changes – rather one phase develops out of the one before and traces of a former permeate the latter. Also, Piaget's stage theory has been criticised by researchers who found that the adult language he used in his tests might have obscured what the children really knew. When these tests were repeated using child-friendly language the children were found to be able to 'conserve' (to keep a mental image in their heads and not be misled by visual cues), and to understand the perspective of others, at earlier ages than the age of 7 years he had suggested.

Q. Could the developments of all these competences – movement, language and play – be linked in some way?

Certainly, as muscle strength develops, children are enabled to do more things. This applies to both fine and gross motor skills. They need to develop control of the soft palate, lips and tongue before they can articulate words clearly; and once they can do this, they are able to express their intentions and wishes in play situations. Every action requires a level of co-ordination, which comes from muscle control. Table 9.1 is an attempt to link aspects of development in a time-frame. However, some children will travel at unequal speeds and some will have a more uneven pattern of development than others.

Q. If the children speak early and reach their 'motor' milestones ahead of time, does this mean they are 'intelligent' and will do well all through school?

When results of the first IQ tests for early years children were followed up, they showed little prognostic accuracy. Perhaps they were too limited in the competences they tried to measure or perhaps so many other variables affected the children that the scores were not useful. Today, especially with older children, the scores do seem to allow more accurate assessments, but still need to be regarded with caution, as there can be some variation. For this reason, it is only the extremes of low and high competence that would be measured as routine, because exceptional scores would need additional teaching input.

Q. Why should it all be so difficult?

First of all, let's look at the concept of intelligence. With language and physical development, intelligence has a genetic link: temperament can influence attitudes to new learning so this is important as well as scores in IQ tests. But the environment also plays a major part in terms of the opportunities and experiences the children have and how these contribute both to confidence and to general knowledge.

IQ tests really resulted from research that was looking at reasons for the variations in children's capacities to solve problems, to use alternative strategies and to embrace new learning. It sought to measure these differences in order to make prognoses about children's development and appropriate education. The range of IQ scores varies from below 60 (these children need additional support), to 100 (this group would be described as 'average'), to 130–140 or even higher (these children need extended learning opportunities or, if deemed best, acceleration). Within this gifted group there are children who are 'good at everything'. Sometimes called 'garden-variety gifted', they tend to fit in with their peers better than those gifted children who are way beyond the norm in one particular area (these children may find it difficult to interact at the correct level with their peers and they may show more emotional problems).

Of course, the IQ scores can only reflect the competences that were tested, and the realisation that children had a whole range of different strengths has led to different models of intelligence. Arguably the best known is Gardner's (1983) research, which defined six different intelligences: linguistic, musical, logical-mathematical, spatial, bodily kinaesthetic and personal. However, all the different models spelt out the important fact that 'IQ tests failed to measure important qualities that could stand the children in good stead beyond the confines of the school'.

Q. What about talented children?

In 2001, several new publications separated 'giftedness' and 'talent'. One, 'A Framework for Gifted and Talented Pupils' (City of Edinburgh Council, 2001) defined giftedness as 'the possession of untrained and spontaneously expressed natural ability, in at least one ability domain to a degree that places the young person in the top 15 per cent of his age group'. In contrast, they defined talent as achievement in any field of performance. The talented pupils, they explained, were performing at a level significantly beyond what one might expect for their age, but this had come about by sustained rigorous practice built upon interest, enthusiasm and talent.

This document claims that 'quality early years provision has the potential for satisfying gifted and talented youngsters'. However, it also urges practitioners to identify these children, to build relationships with their parents and to build a full profile of competences as a basis for planning further learning.

Q. What kinds of activities would suit able children?

Perhaps they could use a digital camera to take outside photographs, then arrange their pictures to illustrate a story they will tell to a small group? Or practitioners could make up a parcel with foreign stamps and use that as a basis for discussion: 'Where has it come from? Who sent it? What could be inside? Who is it for?', and so on. A similar activity could ensue if the children found a toy animal with a notice saying 'Please help me' under a tree in the garden (rather like Paddington Bear). The children could discuss what foods they should provide, where he would sleep, what he was to be called and who would be his friend. Or children could fill a small box of things they have made to sell at a parents' evening. The proceeds would go to children overseas. Such episodes encourage the development of imaginative thinking, and altruism too!

Q. And what about children with additional learning needs?

Rather like the gifted and talented differentiation, it is important to identify whether children have a specific learning difficulty, where one aspect of their development is at a much lower level than the others, but where this is unexpected given their other strengths. Such children are likely to need specialised support to compensate for their difficulties, but can do very well in academic work. Children with a global developmental delay find learning across the board problematic and they need help in all aspects of their learning. In 2014 after inclusion has been adopted as a key educational strategy, many more children with physical and intellectual difficulties have been moved into mainstream education. However, unless adequate specialised support is provided, they may flounder. Inclusion means very much more than simply being together under the same roof. If the strengths of an inclusive model are to be realised, then resources, in terms of trained personnel and equipment, must match the children's needs. Unfortunately, there are areas where the rhetoric does not yet match the reality.

Thankfully, in the early years setting, the higher staff/pupil ratio allows intervention at the correct time and at the most appropriate level; and the play-based curriculum allows all children to cope at their own level. This is very good news.

Q. How can we convince parents that children are learning as they play? They are often overly anxious that their child learns facts and develops specific skills such as writing when the children are not ready for this kind of input.

That question is really important. After all practitioners have studied play and all the competences it promotes but most parents have not had this opportunity. There are different ways to pass on this information. While posters and charts can be time consuming to make, they do convey the analysis that has preceded the selection of areas or corners and the competences that would form the topics for observation and assessment. Parents can study them at their leisure and ask questions/suggest additions or amendments. They can then feel part of their child's learning programme and begin to understand the subtleties and benefits of learning.

Another possibility would be to have a photo of children engaged in a shared learning activity (Figure 9.3) with the learning competences listed below.

Such a photo would be a good introduction to discuss with parents because the learning competences are fairly easily identified. Also this is quite a familiar scene and parents will identify more easily with this kind of task than siphoning water or large construction.

The children are learning the preparation that precedes handling food (hands washed, aprons on). They are working in a group so sharing resources. This may mean waiting and taking turns. They are producing tea for someone else and so are involved in an unselfish act (developing altruism and empathy). They are developing motor skills (manipulative skills) through spreading the toast – learning how hard butter is difficult to spread.

They are learning table manners and the skills of daily living e.g. preparing and serving food and sitting at table to eat together. Perhaps some of the children will pour water, juice or milk, and ask the others which one they would prefer.

The learning is more subtle when Ben learns to trundle a tyre. Ben is learning:

- To keep his balance as he pushes the tyre. This means adjusting his stance and concentrating his efforts.
- To gauge how much strength is needed and what happens when he uses too little or too much.

155

FIGURE 9.3 Teatime

- How to use his right, dominant hand for pushing and sending the tyre in the right direction.
- About safety, i.e. not pushing the tyre near other children.
- How much speed is needed to keep the tyre moving and what happens when the strength and speed dissipate (the tyre falls over). Then he can suggest what else to do with the tyre e.g. sit/bounce on it/fill it with sand or earth as a planter.

FIGURE 9.4 Ben and the tyre

- About the tread and how it helps the tyre to cling to the road. He can investigate how many kinds of transport use tyres like this.

So within these two play activities there is social, emotional, movement and intellectual learning. Placing the children's learning in context like this can explain the purpose of learning through play. This can be a difficult thing to do.

When parents are well informed, it is so much easier for practitioners and parents to work together. They then recognise that their aim is the same, i.e. to have each child enjoy learning, each one able to share any worries, each one able to learn confidence and develop a positive self-esteem. Surely that is what true learning is all about?

The motor milestones

Age	Locomotor skills	Nonlocomotor skills	Manipulative skills
Birth	Primitive walking reflex and swimming reflex but these will disappear.	Will focus at feeding distance: hold eye contact.	May hold finger for a moment.
4 months	Can sit (briefly) if propped up. Enjoys baby massage and tummy time.	Plays with hands as first toy: will hold object briefly; head should be steady, handgrip firm.	First attempts at passing objects from hand to hand. Plays with toes – puts toes in mouth.
6–9 months	Crawls speedily; some children pulling up to stand: Sense of danger evident (2 weeks after crawling).	Sitting without support. Reaching and grasping more accurately now.	Holds toys; feeds self with bottle or finger food. Recognises that dropped objects are still there – seeks to retrieve them.
9–12 months	Crawling, walking round furniture, crawling up stairs.	Shows preference for some toys; handles them carefully.	Scribbles holding pencil firmly. Everything to the mouth for testing texture and taste.
12–18 months	Walking securely. Will roll over and crawl as a combined action. Rhythmic 'dancing' to music.	Does simple puzzles; uses the pincer grip. Enjoys knocking toys over; cares for soft toys – first signs of shared empathy.	Will turn the pages of books. Independent feeding. Uses 2 hands independently.

Age	Locomotor skills	Nonlocomotor skills	Manipulative skills
18–24 months	Runs (20 mo), walks well (24 mo); climbs stairs with both feet on each step.	Pushes and pulls boxes or wheeled toys; unscrews lid on a jar.	Shows clear hand preference; stacks 4 to 6 blocks; turns pages one at a time; picks things up without overbalancing.
2–3 years	Runs easily. Climbs up, down and over obstacles unaided.	Enjoys drawing and painting with large brush.	Picks up small objects (e.g. cheerios). Throws small ball forward while standing.
3–4 years	Walks upstairs one foot per step; skips using alternate feet; walks on tiptoe.	Pedals and steers a tricycle: Walks in any direction pulling a big toy: Rotates body when throwing but still little body rotation.	Catches large ball between outstretched arms; cuts paper with scissors; holds pencil between thumb and first two fingers.
4–5 years	Walks up and downstairs one foot per step; stands, runs and walks well. Combines actions seamlessly e.g. run and jump.	Boys show mature throwing action. Girls enjoy balance challenges such as ballet.	Strikes ball with bat; kicks and catches ball; threads beads but not needle; grasps pencil maturely.
5–6 years	Skips on alternate feet; walks a thin line; slides, swings.	More children show mature turning and kicking action.	Plays ball games quite well. Threads needle and sews stitches.

A developmental plan for speaking

Age	Words	Stories	Activities
5 years	Clear articulation; compound phrases.	Can retell a story; suggest new ideas. Can sequence three pictures. Uses pronouns now. May read single words. Likes to have scribing of own ideas done.	Can empathise with others' feelings; understands rules and routines.
4 years	Seeks explanations. Asks When? Why? Can visualise events elsewhere.	Enjoys repetition and contributing known phrases to stories. Can retell a story or invent one.	Can role play. Can understand characterisation.
3 years	Uses sentences of 4–5 words. Complex use of words.	Will listen, adapt and recast sentences. Uses 'why?' constantly. Plays with nonsense words and rhymes.	Joins in songs and rhymes. Beats rhythms. Enjoys drawing with coloured chalks.
2 years	Huge increase in vocabulary – the naming explosion. Links two words e.g. love you, go away.	Follows stories – recognises favourite characters and routines. Gesture and body language combined – holophrases. Communication strategies used e.g. motherese (higher pitched simplified language).	Asserts independence – has tantrums. Telegraphic speech, i.e. uses only essential words, e.g. 'I going'.

Age	Words	Stories	Activities
1 year	Monosyllabic babbling; da, da, da. Understanding evident from facial expression and gestures.	Understands simple instructions, e.g. come here; can convey wishes through gestures. Understands 50 words; makes own words for wants. Words learned slowly at this pre-linguistic stage.	Enjoys peep-boo (the basis of turn taking). Memory and a sense of self are developing.
3–9 months	Controls gestures; joint attention beginning to develop.	Beginning to understand several words. Babbling dadadada on request	Uses smiling to good effect. Claps hands; beginning to point.
Birth–3 months	Cries, increasingly with meaning.	Beginning to communicate with gurgles. Coo-ing.	Recognises familiar people as source of comfort.

Bibliography

Ainsworth, M. (1972) 'Attachment and dependency: a comparison' in J.L. Gerwirtz (ed.) *Attachment and Dependency*. Washington, DC: VH Winston.

Bakker, D.J. (1990) *Neurophysiological Treatment of Dyslexia*. New York: Oxford University Press INC.

Bee, H. (2002) *The Developing Child*. New York: HarperCollins College Publishers.

Bee, H. (2004) *The Growing Child*. New York: HarperCollins College Publishers.

Bee, H. (2010) *The Developing Child* (10th edn). New York: HarperCollins College Publishers.

Bee, H. and Boyd, D. (2005) *The Developing Child* (international edition). Boston MA: Pearson Publications.

Bellhouse, B., Johnson, J. and Fuller, F. (2005) *Empathy: Promoting Resilience and Emotional Intelligence for Young People Aged 7–11*. London: Lucky Duck Publishing/Paul Chapman.

Bowlby, J. (1988) *A Secure Base: Clinical Applications of Attachment Theory*. London: Routledge.

Carter, R. (2000) *Mapping the Mind*. London: Phoenix Books.

City of Edinburgh Council (2001) *A Framework for Gifted and Talented Pupils*. Edinburgh: City of Edinburgh Council.

Cohen, D. (1990) *The Development of Play*. New York: New York University Press.

Collins, M. (2005) *It's OK to be Sad. Activities to Help Children Manage Loss, Grief and Bereavement*. London: Lucky Duck Publishing/Paul Chapman.

Davies, G. and Cummings, E.M. (1994) 'Marital conflict and child adjustment'. *Psychological Bulletin*, 116, 387–411.

Dowling, M. (2004) *Young Children's Personal, Social and Emotional Development*. London: Paul Chapman.

Dyspraxia Foundation (2001) *Report: Praxis Makes Perfect*. Hitchin: Dyspraxia Foundation.

Eisenberg, N. (1990) *The Development of Prosocial Behaviour*. Hillsdale, NY: Erlbaum.

Eisenberg, N. (1992) *The Caring Child*. Cambridge, MA: Harvard University Press

Francis, P.L., Self, P.A. and Horowitz F.D. (1987) 'The behavioural assessment of the neonate'. An overview in I.D. Osofsky (ed.) *Handbook of Infant Development* (2nd edn), pp. 723–779. New York: Wiley-Interscience.

Gardner, H. (1983) *Frames of Mind: The Theory of Multiple Intelligences*. New York: Basic Books.

Goddard, S. (1996) *A Teacher's Window into the Child's Mind*. Eugene, OR: Fern Ridge Press.

Goddard S. (2002) *Reflexes, Learning and Behavior*. Eugene, OR: Fern Ridge Press.

Isaacs, S. (1933) *Social Development in Young Children*. London: Routledge.

Katz, L.F. and Gotttman, J.M. (1993) 'Patterns of marital conflict predict children's internalising and externalising behaviours'. *Developmental Psychology*, 29, 940–950.

Kohlberg, L. (1969) 'Stages and sequence: the cognitive-developmental approach to socialisation' in D.A. Goslin (ed.) *Handbook of Socialisation Theory and Research*. Chicago, IL: Rand McNally.

Lewis, T.L., Amini, F. and Lannon, R. (2010) *A General Theory of Love*. New York: Vintage.

Maccoby, E. and Martin, E (1990) 'Socialisation in the context of the family' in E.M. Hetherington (ed.) *Handbook of Child Psychology* vol. 4. New York: Wiley.

Macintyre, C. (2003) *Jingle Time*. London: David Fulton Publishers.

Macintyre, C. (2010) *Play for Children with Special Needs* (2nd edn). Abingdon: Routledge.

Macintyre, C. (2011) *Understanding Babies and Young Children from Conception to Three. A Guide for Students, Practitioners and Parents*. London: Routledge.

Macintyre, C. (2012) *Enhancing Learning through Play* (2nd edn). Abingdon: Routledge.

Macintyre, C. (2014) *Identifying Additional Learning Needs in the Early Years* (2nd edn). London: Routledge.

Macintyre, C. and Mcvitty, K. (2003) *Planning the Pre-5 Setting*. London: David Fulton Publishers.

163

Macintyre, C. and McVitty, K. (2004) *Movement and Learning in the Early Years*. London: Sage/Paul Chapman Publishing.

Melhuish, E.C. (1990) *Research on Day Care for Young Children in the United Kingdom: International Perspectives.* London: Routledge.

Moore, C. (2012) *George and Sam.* London: Penguin Books

Murray, M. and Keene, C. (1998) *The ABC of Bullying.* Dublin: Mercier Press.

Myers, B.J. (1999) 'Mother–infant bonding. The status of this critical period hypothesis.' *Developmental Review*, 4, 240–278.

Naisbitt, A.E. (2001) *Creating the Inclusive Classroom: Meeting the Needs of Gifted and Talented Children in the Mainstream Classroom.* Redcar: Cleveland Publications.

Paley, V.G. (2004) *A Child's Work. The Importance of Fantasy Play*. Chicago UL: University of Chicago Press.

Palmer, S. (2006) *Toxic Childhood.* London: Orion Books.

Piaget, J. (1932) *The Moral Judgement of the Child.* Harmondsworth: Penguin.

Piaget, J. (1954) *The Construction of Reality in the Child.* New York: Basic Books.

Pinker, S. (1994) *The Language Instinct: How the Mind Creates Language.* New York: William Morow.

Robinson, M. (2011) *Understanding Behaviour and Development in Early Childhood. A Guide to Theory and Practice.* London: Routledge.

Schafffer, H.R. (1990) *Social Development.* Oxford: Blackwell Publishing.

Sutherland, M. (2008) *The Key Relational Need of the Child.* Paper presented at the North East Special Needs Conference, Bolden.

Sutherland, M. (2006) *The Science of Parenting.* New York: Dorling Kindersley.

Trevarthen C. (1977) *Play for Tomorrow.* Video production, University of Edinburgh.

Winston, R. (2004) *The Human Mind.* New York: Bantam Books.

Winston, R. (2006) *Child of Our Time.* Television series for BBC1.

Index